DEMOFARE

Lyne and John

PAUL WANDRUM

Paul Wandrum

This paperback edition published 2023 by Paul Wandrum Author

an imprint of Paul Wandrum Author Publishing

Paisley, Scotland

ISBN: 978-1-7392119-0-5

Email PaulWandrumAuthor@gmail.com to find out about all our books and to purchase them. You will also find features, author information and news of any events, also be the first to hear about our new releases.

Acknowledgements

I would like to thank my sister Megan for all her hard work promoting this book on social media and technical help. I truly could not have done it without her and also my brother Joseph who took his time to create some very cool graphic concepts. To my little red-haired nephew Myles who is always so crazy and hyper.

A massive thank you also to the team at Jasami Publishing. To Douglas O'Hara for his support and editing to turn Demons Fare into the novel it is. To Michèle Smith for her constant support and encouraging words from start to finish, and lastly to Raquel Alemán Cruz for taking the time to ensure this novel is perfect for you the reader.

To my partner Lynsey, and three kids who have taught me how to enjoy life again. I look forward to what the future brings.

For the amazing cover you see a massive thank you to Olivia Pro Design. Also a massive thank you to Dian Triyasa for the wonderful illustrations featured throughout.

Finally, for my Uncle John, who always complimented me on my perseverance on doing my writing every morning.

Dedications

To my Mum and Dad, who's love and memories I carry forever. You are both in my heart until we meet again.

This book is also dedicated to my Nana and Papa who were a big part of my life and shaped me into the man I am.

Lastly, to the Late Kevin Ritchie, the best family friend there was.

Table of Contents

Prologue

The Cathedral Eagle

Beyond the ornate quire screen of the Glasgow Cathedral is the home of the Eagle Lectern — standing proudly with its wooden wings flared and its eyes scowling. Every year visitors and worshippers marvel at its elegant, seventeenth- century French design, but not cleaning attendant Peggy Bain, no way. For eight years now she has had her morning housekeeping job at the cathedral, and that big, auld birdy has always given her an unsettling feeling, as if its sullen eyes stared back at her, tracking her every movement.

Most mornings, she would leave off putting her blue feather duster to it until the very end of her shift — swearing it would angrily whisper some sort of gibberish. Her husband had thought she had been inhaling a few too many cleaning supplies when she told him, and maybe he had a point. She had been working double shifts for the last year to keep up with the bills. In fact, that's exactly what she thought until last Tuesday, when she noticed the ghastly bird of prey had been gradually shedding more and more wood chippings onto the cathedral floor each day.

After avoiding the bird for a few days, Peggy had finally had enough. At the end of her next morning shift, she mustered up enough courage to not only dust the bird, but to examine its cold, judging eyes for more than a moment. She returned her feathered duster into the pocket of her red tabard apron and glanced at her wristwatch. Two minutes to eleven.

"Alright, eagle eyes," she said, slightly timid. "Let me have a wee look at why you're beginning to chip so I can report it to Reverend Mark." She inched closer to its face, studying the bird. "Hopefully you're damaged enough for him to lock ye away in the storage cupboard and out of my sight for good."

What Peggy didn't know was that a horrendous evil trapped inside the wooden bird had reawakened. After a long slumber, it was hungry for revenge.

Peggy was brushing her fingers across a chipped piece near the back of the bird's head when a brief snapping sound, like a box of matchsticks breaking, came from the bird's eye sockets. Peggy stepped back and watched as fragments of wood fell onto the ground, then glanced quickly back at the bird's eyes and the crackling stopped. Then, in one piece, the eagle's beak broke cleanly off and fell to the floor. Before Peggy had the chance to look down at where it landed, her whole body tensed and froze with fear.

Protruding from the eagle's beak was a pale, almost translucent skin and a single charcoal-coloured eye peeking through and staring at her. Peggy stepped back, her hands shaking. The bird stretched its wings and lifted itself from the lectern and away from its sphere-column perch. The eagle took flight, circling the room once and, with an intense fury, tucked its wings closer to its chest and smashed straight through the blue stained-glass window of Moses and into the city of Glasgow.

Part I

The Return of Terry Doyle

One

As the train screeched to a stop, Terry Doyle glanced outside the smudged, stained window and realised he had finally arrived back in his home city of Glasgow for the first time in ten years. Hovering by the train doors, he cautiously scanned the groups of people manoeuvring through the station, searching for the slightest hint of her presence. A feeling of paranoia and fear lingered in his mind as he planted both feet firmly on the train, unsure if he had made the right decision coming home. He took a step back and felt a herd of people behind him pressing against him. Before he knew it, the eager passengers had nudged him forward onto the station platform, and the decision had been made. He inhaled a long, deep breath and reluctantly made his way toward the auld station clock.

He was there to meet Pastor Hugh McClelland, the spiritual leader of the church he used to attend regularly with his wife and kids back in the days when he still had a family. As Terry shuffled past a few eager passengers, he was pleased to notice Hugh was already waiting. His head of hair, which used to be a thick jet-black and styled like a king of rock 'n' roll, was now greying at the sides. To Terry's surprise, Hugh seemed to still possess the same habit of tucking his cigarette behind his right ear. It was a subtle observation and one that recalled a sense of normalcy akin to the one he had before his involuntary departure.

"Now, don't tell me you're still smoking those cancer sticks whilst saying your prayers to our good Lord, are ye, Hugh?" Terry asked, smiling as he walked towards his auld friend and possibly the only man that could help him survive being back in the city for at least a day.

"Now that you mention it, I was actually just praying to him, hoping you hadn't gotten any uglier than what you were a decade ago." Hugh's dark brown eyes studied him with a confident yet friendly look. "Well, big man, you're unlucky, I suppose. Guess the Lord works in mysterious ways. Look at me, I haven't changed a bit, eh?"

"Not a bit," Terry grinned.

The two men hugged under the auld clock as many friends, lovers and even enemies had done in times gone by. It had been so long since Terry had felt the comfort of a friend and the sound of a familiar voice. He gripped Hugh tighter and fought the surge of tears cresting around his eyes. *I want to tell him. I want to tell him the full story right here and now. I want to break down and just fucking cry my demons out until he tells me it's alright and that I'm safe. Safe to finally come back home to my family, where I belong.*

"Right, big chap, less of the bloody waterworks before we get on the bus back to Millers Park Church. May God forgive me for swearing, but trust me, mate, you don't want to have a meltdown in front of all those nosey bastards. Do you know what I mean, aye?"

"Aye, I do know what ye mean," said Terry, wiping his coat sleeve across his eyes. "Good to see you're still the foul-mouthed, tough-as-nails Glaswegian pastor."

Hugh shrugged. "I'm always forgiven … eventually." His once happy face transformed into a deep, foreboding stare as thoughts of his past crept to the forefront of his mind. "Let's just hope you feel better when we get back there." He wrapped his arm around Terry, his face easing back to normal. "Now, come on, we better hurry and catch this bus, mate. Hopefully we can be at the church for a quarter to ten."

Both men walked down the stairs at the Union Street exit and out of the station onto the bustling streets of Glasgow. Terry's eyes narrowed, examining every passerby with an intense caution. "I know it may sound odd," Terry said. "But it's better we stay clear of Hope Street. Just in case she knows I'm back. I don't want to risk it."

The desperation and fear in Terry's voice caused an unnerving paranoia in Hugh's mind. His auld friend had been frightened to his core. Despite his reservations about Terry's whereabouts, even at that moment, he considered something bad could be waiting behind a corner. Nobody just goes to work one night and then disappears. Hugh firmly believed the Lord worked in mysterious ways, and today he simply couldn't wait to unravel the mystery of how this man just vanished ten years ago to the day on December 6th, 2009.

Both men took their seats at the back of the bus, away from any curious eavesdroppers. As the bus hissed forward, Hugh grabbed the back of the seat in front of him and turned toward Terry. "Now, when we get there, you're absolutely sure you're ready to stand up in front of around thirty people and tell them your story?"

Without hesitation, Terry turned toward his friend, filled with purpose. "I have to, Hugh, for more reasons than one. I'll tell you all everything right from the beginning. I need to do it, mate ... I need to try and repair my soul while I still have time."

"Alrighty then, son. You'll probably notice some of the auld faces have changed over the years. Then again, somehow time doesn't seem to have aged you, Terry, but for goodness' sake, just don't confess to us you've been sunning it up in the bloody Florida Keys all this time."

"Let's just say I went to someplace that was a hundred times more roasting than Florida, that's for sure," Terry said, turning toward the window.

Both men fell silent for the rest of the journey to Millers Park. As the bus turned down a narrow street lined with parked cars, Pastor Hugh stole a quick glance at Terry without him noticing. Here was the man who had gone out to start his usual night shift driving his hackney cab and never returned. Hugh remembered the times when, as the days turned into weeks, Terry's wife, Anne, would phone the house every day and every night asking if he had heard any news. He had let her down easy for the first few weeks until about a month into the investigation, when the police had discovered his black hackney cab in Glasgow's Queen Mary Avenue — parked outside an ill-omened house, the former residence of university professor John Dunlop and his lecturer wife Trisha. The couple had tragically lost their lives when the building caught fire in 1976. Many suspected the house had been cursed, but no legitimate connection had been made to Terry's disappearance. The inside of his vehicle had been clean and suggested nothing out of the ordinary, and eventually the trail went cold. It was as if Terry Doyle never existed.

Just what in God's name happened to you that night, Terry? Hugh thought as the bus passed by a graffitied signpost which slightly obscured the name: MILLERS PARK. *And just what did ye mean last night on the phone?* Hugh recalled Terry's words with a shudder. *"Demons walk silently amongst us, Hugh, and most of the time we just don't know it. Once you hear my story tomorrow you will know."*

Two

I t had been during last night's mysterious phone call that Terry Doyle had finally got back in touch with not only his former spiritual mentor, but also his truest friend after a decade.

Now, the two men were getting off a bus together at the corner of West Millers Avenue and heading towards an eighteenth-century red sandstone building that was Millers Park Christian Community Church Hall. A barrage of worrying thoughts plagued Pastor Hugh as he walked slightly ahead of Terry and squeaked open the freshly crimson-painted iron gates with their dangerously sharp and almost unwelcoming arrowed spikes.

"You will remember this auld gate well, eh?" Hugh asked whilst undoing the padlock.

"I do indeed," said Terry, his voice crumbling to a whisper. "I remember the very first day my Anne brought me down here to meet you. Our David must've been only about five at the time … Do ye remember how he started greetin just at the sight of this gate?"

"He thought you were taking him to a haunted house."

"Aye, that he did," said Terry, grinning reminiscently at the faded memory of what felt like a previous life.

They both climbed the first couple of steps leading to the church's entrance. It was an arched doorway with two faded engravings on either side. On the right, a saint-like figure with a halo held a cross-shaped item in one hand and a fiery torchlight in the other, while, on the left, an engraved creature resembled a large demonic bat with horns.

Terry stood directly between both, and wondered what image called to him more these days. He wished to confess to Hugh exactly what the engravings meant, but that would be like revealing to someone who loves life that they may just have to die a lot sooner than they thought. He was on a mission to heal his soul and to warn those of the coming danger in the days ahead. For a moment, however brief, he wished to spare his friend the news of what evil lurked in the shadows.

Hugh, noticing the pained look in his friend's eyes, continued. "As you might remember me saying once, those gates have been here since the construction of the earlier church building way back in 1771."

Terry pulled himself away from the gate and nodded. "That's very impressive, Hugh, you should look into writing something about the building, ye know. They might even publish it in the local history section of the paper, people love buildings and monuments with a story."

"A story just like you have today, aye?" asked Hugh, his tone unconvinced. He furrowed his brow and glared down at Terry on the step below him.

"Well … aye," said Terry, sounding slightly angered and defensive. "It's not made up, Hugh. How are ye needing me to try and assure you my story is a true one?

"You haven't assured me of nothing, pal, and beyond these doors at approximately half ten will be the big audience you asked for … which may also include your former wife and boy."

After hearing these harsh words from his best friend and mentor, Terry came to a sudden halt on the steps. He then finally decided to ask the question he had been dreading an answer to since he stepped off the train. "For a man whom I once knew to have a lot of faith in me, you don't believe a word that comes out of my mouth anymore, do ye, Hugh?"

Hugh stared at the look of emptiness and loss in the eyes of the man he was trying to fully trust but couldn't. Nothing made sense. Everything pulled at the faith he once had for his friend.

"Go ahead, then," Terry continued. "Tell me to my face that you think I'm lying. You have changed for the worse, you used to never hold things back years ago," Terry said in a voice that was now beginning to break with disappointment.

"Look, I don't think you're completely lying, but–"

"Nah, ye do, Hugh. Back when I joined this church, you told me to always tell the truth and shame the devil. Well, that is what I am here to do today. Not for my sake, but for everyone's. You all need to be warned. You don't know the things I've seen. The things which would drive others mad. I'm shattered you're not taking this seriously yet, but–"

"Aw, come off it, son, will ye?" Pastor Hugh yelled at him the way any da does when trying to deal with a boy that has gone off the rails. Terry hadn't exactly looked at Hugh as a father figure, he never had, but more as a wiser big brother he secretly wanted to replicate. Hugh leaned closer and looked around cautiously so no one was in earshot. "I mean, God forgive us, I hate using words like these, but for fuck's sake, man, can ye actually hear yourself, Terry?"

"Why, wits the matter, are ye just praying the story I tell in there isn't going to be some made-up sob story I put together to mask some mid-life crisis love affair I must have been having?" Terry said, his voice raised.

Hugh threw down his set of clunky keys and pointed an accusatory finger at Terry. "Well, wit in the name a fuck are we all supposed to think? I mean, you just phone me out of the blue, and ye expect me to be the answer to all your prayers? To accept what little of this story you've mentioned? Did you know that, after you vanished, we spent six long years trying to find out what might have happened to you?"

Terry lowered his head. "Look, Hugh, I'm grateful for all—"

"Just shut it and listen. Even when the polis gave up after two and a half years, every member of this church, including myself, Gloria and that wonderful woman you used to have the great privilege of calling your wife, never gave up hope, pal." Hugh picked up his keys and clutched them tightly in his hand. "I sure hope this story of yours heals the rift you put between everyone you loved, Terry. Because your Anne and your boy were in bits after you left. I mean, come on, as if they hadn't just been through enough after your wee Shauna passed away. God rest her," he said, making the sign of the cross.

"For the last time and for the love of …" Terry paused, rubbing his forehead as though contracting a bad migraine. "I never just decided one night to run away from my family, Hugh. If you and Gloria and every good Christian member who attends this morning will just hear me out, I am sure you will understand that I simply had nae choice in the matter."

Three

Inside, Terry stared ominously at the statue of the Lord on the cross near the sermon altar, knowing what evil he had hidden there all those years ago. He shifted his focus as Hugh looked back at him and stared at the floor he had helped him retile a decade ago. Seeing the church incurred a wave of flashbacks. The weekly conversations over a cup of tea with fellow members after the service, volunteering for the church food bank, and happily bringing his boy and late daughter to weekly Sunday school. They were happy in this house of God, saying their prayers and singing along, loud and proud, to some of the Christian rock bands Hugh would let play on Thursday nights. Terry knew exactly what he wanted out of being born again all those years ago and he loved the new life he made with it. He knew some people might think of them as an odd bunch, but to hell with them, they were happy, and, most of all, they were good people.

As they walked past the stained-glass windows, which were letting in a faint glow of light, Terry glanced at the rows of pews and then the altar at the opposite end of the church. "Oh, and not to worry, Hugh. I remembered your auld house rules of speaking confidently during a church talk. Speak loud and clear, don't trip over the furniture and make sure my fly's up," he said, trying to break the silence between them.

He hoped Hugh would return at least half a laugh or a smile back at him for remembering this, but all he said was, "Give me a hand to set up."

About twenty minutes later, Terry recited the Lord's Prayer in his head before nervously making his way to the microphone stand he and Hugh had set up next to the pastor's podium under the huge engraving of Jesus on the cross. The born-again folks were now pouring into the building to get a seat, though there was no sign of David or Anne. However, as he cleared his throat and readied himself to speak, Terry noticed some familiar faces. Ronald Fergus, a local gardener; Katherine Bills; and his old next-door neighbours, Teresa and James Dickson, who helped him and his wife carry their wee girl's coffin, and who now sat looking straight at the floor and avoided his gaze.

"Good morning, everyone, thank you for coming out and thanks again to Pastor Hugh for allowing me to do this today. My name is Terry Doyle and some of you, of course, might remember me from when I used to attend this very church with my family."

"Here, Doyle, you must have some brass neck on ye, mate, thinking ye can just swagger back here and expect everybody to believe some shite story!" someone shouted from the row of seats furthest back.

Terry opened his mouth to reply, but, before he could, Hugh lifted from his seat and addressed the congregation. "Right, folks, I think it's important we get the chance to properly hear first what the man is trying to tell us without any holier than thou numpty's shouting out stuff." Hugh glanced at Terry for a moment as if to apologise for not doing the same.

Terry nodded back at his auld friend, and then addressed the audience. "Now, my good people, if you will allow me the chance to tell you all the truth of how I really vanished ten years ago this very night. Or, as we all say here at church, the truth the way God sees it ..."

Part II

Ten Years Ago, Tonight

Four

On the night I disappeared, I had been in my taxi outside Glasgow Central Station as usual, waiting for my next fare and listening to my Eagles CD. The majestic voice of Glenn Frey was ironically singing *One of These Nights* as heavy droplets of April rain hammered against my cabbie's roof. At first, all seemed normal. I noticed an older gentleman, well wrapped up in a wee tammy hat and scarf, dragging his luggage along towards me. Quickly, I gave him the routine wave and thumbs up to signal I was ready to go whenever he was and … that's when she appeared.

She had come from behind this old fella, calmly shoving him out of her way as though the man was nothing more than a cardboard cut-out prop. The auld boy almost decked it, but was thankfully steadied by a young man passing by. Either way, folks, I just couldn't have that at all. I was brought up to respect the elderly, and so I tried doing the decent thing and rolled down my window to get things straightened out.

"Sorry, darlin, but the man ye just barged on past there was before you," I said to her.

"No, wait. Please, I'm bleeding, man," she said, in a tone of piercing panic in between quick, shallow breaths. "You must take me to the royal; my ex has just stabbed me in the middle of the train station."

As usual, I did a lot more panicking instead of thinking. "My goodness … Right, come on and get in. I will get ye there." I roughly recalled these being the words I said through the sudden rush of dread working its way through me. I flicked on the cabbie's lights to notice the young woman clutching her right hand over her stomach as blood, like dark wine, seeped through her fingers and dripped onto her jeans.

"Keep pressure on it. Try and take deep, slow breaths the now, pal, and try not to fall asleep," I said as she struggled to find a position on the seats behind me. "You can even try and lay up on the seats as well, I mean … If you want. I am truly sorry, darlin, but for the life of me I don't really know the proper health and safety protocols for these situations."

"I'm fine, plus, I learned at university …" she said, pausing from the pain.

"Just save your strength and I promise I will get us there as quick as I can, ok?" I eased the cabbie onto Gordon Street, honking for cars to move.

"I'm Lillian, by the way. You're a real hero for doing this."

"We are not there yet, pet. Nae need for thank yous just now," I said, speeding down the street before the light changed.

As reckless of me as it was, I took too much of a sharp turn onto West Nile Street and almost knocked over two intoxicated young guys. By the looks of them, they had just stumbled out of the nearest pub. One of the bigger boozed-up fellas took a free kick at my taxicab door as his pal shouted, calling me a "Fuckin baldy, fat beast". I was used to all sorts of names, being a cabbie driver, but what really surprised me was the sudden outburst of laughter coming from my supposedly injured passenger Lillian.

"Good to see you can still manage to laugh. Personally, I don't think I could in your situation, to be honest."

"Oh, trust me, driver, if you can't have a laugh in this place ye would greet yourself to death. By the devil, it's good to be back in this auld, dear green place, I must say."

When the supposedly bleeding Lillian said this, she strangely sounded a lot less out of puff than when she first got into my taxi. I couldn't fathom why she sounded almost chirpy, and, at that point, I just put it down to shock and delirium from her wound and went back to keeping my eyes on the road.

"Trust me, it won't be long until we're there, darlin. You're doing good," I said as I drove along Portindas Road and then onto Cowcaddens. I sped up the window wipers, as the heavy downpour had now turned into vicious-looking hailstones, the like of which I hadn't seen since I had visited Belarus in Russia years ago for a football match.

"Ye know I can turn the light back on if you want, pal? It may just help a wee bit with the tiredness."

This is when she said something that well and truly chilled me to the bone.

"Perhaps some things are best kept in the dark after all, Terrance Doyle." Her voice dropped lower, becoming as chilling as a graveyard headstone at night. "I know you've been hiding things away in the darkness. Things which belong to me."

After she had said those words, I eased my foot off the peddle as my legs trembled with fear. It felt like some rotten auld can of worms had been opened deep down within my guts. I turned on the taxi's lights to get a proper look at her. To my immediate horror, I saw this creature staring back at me — looking nothing like the beautiful and bleeding smart girl I had just picked up outside Central Station.

This newly transformed Lillian had dark pits for eyes which spewed flicks of ember and long, scraggly raven-black hair with streaks of silver running through it. She reminded me of those spooky Charlie Manson follower girls they arrested at Spahn Ranch after the Tate and Labianca murders in LA in 1969.

As I cautiously examined this strange new passenger, I began to hear the soft voice of my dearly departed foster mother in my head, whispering, "You will see my true self, Terrance Doyle, past the magician's trick. Do not worry yourself, you're in good hands." The voice then shifted to the very man and auld friend who had so mercifully given me a second chance here today. "By putting your faith in Christ, you will also soon begin to see the truth the way God sees it." Hugh's voice repeated the very same thing on the first day I involved myself with this church many years ago.

Whoever she was … or whatever it was glared back at me in the mirror with a nasty, calculating grin that in my mind seemed to say, "Haha I've got ye now, driver." At that very moment, her sophisticated-looking and beige winter coat morphed into a maroon, leather trench coat that looked as though it belonged to the corpse of a long-dead biker hastily unearthed from its grave.

"What are you? You're not bleeding injured, that's for certain." I asked her.

"You'll know soon enough, Mr Doyle. Enjoy the ride." Lillian snapped her fingers, and soon I felt my eyes grow heavy and the image of my steering wheel slowly faded into blackness. Instinctively, I pressed on the breaks whilst experiencing what felt like riding one of those haunted ghost trains at the theme park. That part of the ride where all the lights and sound effects go off and all you're left with are those few wee seconds that make you want to shout something loud just to test your own existence.

The cab mounted a curb and I found myself in complete darkness, desperately hoping to hear somebody shout, "Get off the pavement with that taxi, ya mad bastard!" Sadly, nobody did. My eyes felt glued shut and

I frantically reached around the taxi's door, felt the handle and opened it.

Now that I finally have people to tell this story, I feel more confident saying with all honesty that I literally threw my fat arse out of the cab as it continued rolling on the curb. I thumped hard against the asphalt as a piercing pain immediately coursed up my spine. Lying on the ground as droplets of icy rain dripped across my face, as if a key unlocked a door, my eyes opened as if nothing had happened.

Nearby, I looked over at the taxi as it slowly rolled to a stop at this muddy bit of spare ground nearby. When I got back up onto my feet, I noticed that, apart from my driver side door being ajar and its engine left running, my faithful auld hackney appeared to be fine. The lights were still on and, to my relief, the sense of darkness had gone away. After a few mild seconds of peace, my mind crept with concern about where Lillian had gone, and I wondered if the wicked magic which had slid over me like a veil inside the cab had just been me blacking out. *Was the woman I picked up even real or just a figment of my overly stressed imagination?* It had been a rough week, sure. But could I have conjured up such a scene?

I rubbed the sides of my head, trying to piece fiction from reality. *No, she was real. I picked her up. She was a young lassie. Injured. Bleeding to death. She was real. She was real.*

As frightened as I was, I walked slowly back towards my taxi, rubbing the bottom of my back. *Maybe she's sprayed some sort of chemical inside the cab to force me out? But force me out to do what exactly?*

"Oh Lord, let's hope not," I said softly to myself. The passenger doors had been closed, and I knew there was a strong possibility she could still be inside the taxi. Thoughts of Lillian lying in wait on the floor of the cab like a stalking hyaena, ready to sneak up on me, flashed across my mind.

"Right, listen up," I said with all the confidence I could muster. "If you're still in there, miss, then I would strongly suggest you come out the now. You see, I have the phone my son got me for Father's Day. I'm not the best with technology, but I'm sure I can press '9' three times on this wee thing and ask for the polis." I waited for a moment, but got no response as thunder and lightning bombarded the night sky.

"Look, Lillian, if I can call you that. Just say you're still here and own up to wit ever it was you were up to tonight, and I'll simply let it go," I said, trying my best to sound like a reasoning man rather than the untrusting scared one I had become. "How does that sound? I just want to get back hame … please."

After a few anxiety-ridden seconds with no response, I finally peered into the passenger side and saw the seats were empty — even the bloodstains which dripped onto the seats were gone. Looking around outside, no one was on the street but me. The spooky, Manson-follower-looking girl had vanished.

Opening the passenger door, I climbed into the back seats and searched feverishly for any clues of her disappearance, finding nothing aside from an unpleasant burning smell, like a crackling fire roasting rotten flesh. Despite the smell, I knew it was in my best interest to get myself home. Whoever that freakish lady had been, I'd have happily paid her fare on the hope I never had to see her again.

Feeling a bit more at ease, I was looking forward to telling Anne and my boy all about this crazy night over a tin of Tenants and the huge pizza I planned on picking up. I quickly got back behind the wheel of my hackney and sighed with an overwhelming relief after noticing my keys were still sitting in the ignition.

I steered the taxi safely back onto the road at Cowcaddens and made a left onto a roundabout near Glasgow Caledonian University. As I passed the complex buildings, I thought about my boy David and how impeccably brave he had been that past year, when we had lost our wee Shauna to a rare genetic disease two days after her ninth birthday. As some of you sitting here today may remember, it was an awful year for me and my family. You might recall my auld hackney around the city with images of our forever-smiling daughter decorated onto the cabbie's doors. Missing my family, I wanted nothing more than to come home, hug my son and kiss my wife, but fate had other plans for me — a destination my darkest nightmares could not conceive.

Part III

Lillian and The Great Fire of 1652

Five

Anne, who I notice hasn't come along today, and I had a bit of a big row on the morning of the night I disappeared. It was about why I had kept the enlarged photos of our Shauna smiling through her last days. Although we had lost our wee girl, I still wanted to do something to help raise awareness and money towards the research that went into trying to save rare cases such as hers.

"Oh, aye, using an image of our wee lassie on her deathbed, that's the way to go." Anne slammed the kitchen table. "Honestly, Terry, the almighty Terry. Just wit would we do without you through all of this?" she said as I sat down with her and our boy at the kitchen table.

"It's bloody better than sitting about the house depressed all day doing hee-haw. Hugh and the other church committee members said it's a good start towards us trusting in the Lord's good fight again. I mean, come on, Anne … I know Shauna is gone, but let's raise money whenever we can to help others like our wee girl."

The argument continued for some time until David, God bless him, had had enough of us. I remember him putting his uneaten toast back on his plate and saying, "Arguing all you two going to do now?" He shook his head and got up from the table. "I'm outta here."

What was more terrible is that we both heard him loud and clear but kept on arguing anyway.

"Yip, that's right, Terry. I'm just Shauna's stupid mammy, a daft mammy that stays at home and has done absolutely hee-haw for her wee girl."

"For goodness' sake, I never said you personally never do anything."

"Nah, forget it. Do what ye please and think what you please from now on, Terry Doyle, because I'm simply done caring," she said flatly.

We both somehow dropped into a tense and prolonged silence until I left for work without saying cheerio once again.

Even though our Shauna had so bravely managed to stay with us through what must have been seven months of agony, me and Anne had slowly lost all the love between us. After I left that morning without saying anything, I somehow knew in my heart it was the beginning of the end for us as a family.

I was driving my cabbie back home, heading towards the centre of Glasgow, as I relived that morning's silly but painful argument with Anne and the recent incident with the fare-jumping demon-lady. I knew my emotions and nerves had been all over the place for most of that year, but what I didn't know at that precise moment was that a true demon had me in its arms. As I drove on towards Castle Street, everything shifted. A sudden lightness started in my feet and spread instantly through my body, as if falling from a rollercoaster or a high place. The sensation curled in my stomach and my head became heavy. Buildings and roads melted back in time, fading from view and transforming. I slowed down and stopped at the corner of what was supposed to be St James Road, but everything had changed.

"Where am I?" I asked myself, gripping my steering wheel tighter and shielding myself with my arm from the glaring light.

The surrounding area looked nothing like the Glasgow I had just been driving in minutes ago. On either side of a winding dirt road, rows of potato crops grew neatly in ploughed fields consisting of what looked like the auld rig and furrow pattern from the rudimentary days of farming. Over by one of the farms, a cockerel crowed, and the chimes of a bell rang nine. It was morning there … wherever "there" was.

I opened the taxi door to have a bit of a look about, but a foul smell caused me to instinctively retreat further into the cab. It had been a mixture of rotting vegetables, ammonia and cattle manure which stung my nose, causing a nausea I had only felt after changing David's diaper as a wee baby. I inhaled a deep breath and stepped out of the taxi, closing the door. Instantly, my socks were soaked and, when I looked down to check my shoes, the concrete road I had expected was a boggy country road that led to God knows where.

After several profanities, I wiped the muck from my shoes and noticed what looked like a church way off in the distance.

Well, Terry, looks like that long-overdue nervous breakdown has arrived. Nearest psychiatric hospital for you, pal. I went back and opened the door of my cab again, reached in and grabbed my keys out of the ignition.

Take the keys with you where, Terry? You don't know where you are, son. You're lost. Who knows, maybe you're already sitting in Psycho Ward 4, dressed in a straitjacket and getting lost inside your own head. I quickly quieted my inner voice and ventured forth, hopefully towards some answers.

I had been walking for about ten minutes on a winding road when I realised I had got no closer to the church, but nearer to auld farmhouses thatched with straw and haystack carts. Glancing around, I found not a soul in sight but the puffs of smoke bellowing from scattered chimneys. Examining a woodsman's axe lodged inside a tree trunk, an odd, primal urge came over me, a need to defend myself in a strange land, and I found myself wondering if I would just be needing it.

It's like I've had some kind of major breakdown, and then bloody woken up on the set of Xena: Warrior Princess, which David and I used to watch.

I laughed in the deafening silence, desiring nothing more than to find a funny side to this situation. Alone. Lost. And not a clue where I was headed. A quack of a door, and an eerie sound of footsteps. Coming from the right, an elderly woman in tattered clothes looking altogether agitated approached.

"You, sonny, are trespassing!" she shouted, pointing a feeble, trembling finger at me. "Ye, begone, or may the Devil's wings carry your soul to Hell's fire."

I tossed my hands in surrender, and calmly said, "Sorry, miss, but I just need some directions. I'm not meaning to trespass, honestly."

Her beady eyes, wise with age, continued to scowl at me with suspicion. "Ye have come to the wrong burgh to try sneak thievery. I've seen lads like you be harled screaming to the gallows for conspiring such wickedness in our dear green place. I'll be watching you, thief." She stomped back to her house and slammed the door shut, watching me scornfully through her window.

Once again, this place made me feel unwelcomed. The front door of her wee farmhouse didn't have any of the fairy-tale-like features: no exterior made of gingerbread and no frosting, but it contained the ugly auld witch who, it seemed, would happily tear the fat of my bones for her scorching oven.

I walked towards the next closest building. It was a structure larger in size, resembling the mediaeval drawings from my son's textbooks. In the distance, these dwellings appeared to be scattered throughout the many acres of the bizarre but somehow picturesque land I now found myself lost in.

As I drew closer to the building, I noticed some of the windows had wooden boards nailed over them in a crisscross fashion, whereas others remained windowless and ramshackled. A type of archway appeared to lead into the actual building itself. I inhaled a deep breath and set off in that direction, hoping to find someone normal and friendly who could shed some light on where I was and how I had got there.

Going under the archway felt unnerving, as if I was being watched not by someone, but by something, and, in that moment, I wished I had brought the axe with me. Midway through the tunnel, a gentle finger tapped my shoulder. I turned so quickly a pain shot up my neck before I let out a squeaky scream, which was embarrassing coming from a middle-aged man.

A young woman stood before me, and in a soft yet desperate voice said, "I have come with the master's belt buckles; they've all been cleaned for today, sir. I know Mr Hamilton expects his wash maids to be punctual. May I now please proceed to the house quarters?"

She couldn't have been any older than twenty, although she looked weathered beyond her years — the kind of ageing only ceaseless manual labour offered. Her face was a silky pale in the dimmed light, while her blue eyes were lively and kind. She carried the belt buckles in a wicker-style basket, clutching it tight against her chest as though her life depended on it — which it probably did.

"Awful sorry for getting in your road there," I said, relaxing my shoulders. "I wonder if you could help me a bit with some directions. You see, I have somehow got myself completely lost." I looked back at the light seeping in from outside the archway. "In more ways than one."

"I'm sorry, but I haven't the time. I must really get to Mr Hamilton's estate, or I might not get paid my day's merks. Perhaps when the day's work is done," she said, and frowned. "I really am sorry, but I must be going."

"I understand, but if you could please tell me where I am. I may have lost my bearings or my mind last night at work. Could you perhaps tell me how I can get back onto the motorway from here?"

"Motorway? I don't know your meaning. Please, ma wee family lives on the edges of this burgh. I can't lose my job. I must be going."

"Honestly, I know what it's like to try and bring home a wage. Could you kindly just tell me where I am?"

The young lady stood silent for a moment, then gave me a sort of queer look that slowly became an awkward smile.

"You are in Glasgow Market. Now, please, I must hurry along and get these buckles up to Mr Hamilton's house. He'll be due back soon from this morning's proceedings on the hill." Avoiding my gaze, she stubbornly brushed past me with the wicker basket in her arms and hurried out of the archway.

"You are in Glasgow Market," I muttered to myself. I wanted to break into a run and catch up with her to ask one more question, but she was gone. And so, I continued walking until the path narrowed and led onto several different alleyways with individual wooden signs indicating place names such as VENNEL STREET and MERCHANT CROSS.

The lassie's words cemented true. Everything had fallen into place, but in the most frightening way. From above one of these auld timber houses I saw a small hatch opening just below the roof, and just right beside where I had been walking came a splattering downpour of the most rancid-smelling greenish diarrhoea. Masking the smell with my shirt, I gagged terribly as I watched people walk over it as if it were routine.

From another small alleyway just to my left I saw a few young barefooted boys, dressed in these horribly unclean rags, playing a chasing game of some kind, running with live hens in their hands.

"C'mon, let's run with these all the way to the Gorbills field," shouted a lanky boy.

"No, let's see if the big ones can swim in the Molendinar Burn. That'll bloody teach auld scat head to take away our spinning tops and game dice," shouted another as they sprinted off in the direction of what appeared to be a rickety, wooden bridge over a small stream, where I could see the cathedral-type building lording on the hill.

The smallest of the boys had this sort of pageboy hairstyle and appeared no older than ten. He had been the slowest of the lot, trying to keep with the others until he took quite a tumble and dropped the plump hen along with some apples he had pinched.

Thinking I was doing the right thing, I cornered the bird and fetched it for him, hoping to trade it for information. It had been a couple of feet away from me anyway, and so I reached down and snatched it up into my arms quite easily. "Hello, young man," I said, as he suspiciously eyed me up and down. "I'm guessing this big mother of a hen was difficult to run with, probably because you're not supposed to steal livestock and run like the clappers with them."

The boy's stringy eyebrows dipped into an angry glare. "Give me that back, or I'll get my gang of merry lads to come back here and take something from you."

"Oh, aye, you and your gang of merry clowns, you mean. Remind me, is that the very same gang who just ran off, leaving behind their smallest clown?"

The boy stomped his foot into the ground. "Give me my bloody hen back, ya big old wart toad," he said, then lunged at me, grappling for the hen in my hands.

"Come, now, there's nae need for such aggressive antics. Look, I'll give you this hen back, but I need a wee bit of a favour in return."

The boy crossed his arms indignantly and said, "Fine by me, toad face. But if this involves me having to go back and steal you more hens or chickens, then it's going to cost ye at least four merks."

"That's a tempting offer, son," I said, even though I hadn't the foggiest idea of what kind of bizarre currency he wanted.

"Look, this is going to sound a bit mad, but I just need you to tell me what year it is."

"That's it?" The boy's face lightened. "I think we got ourselves a deal, sir." He pointed towards the ground. "Today we stand at Glasgow Cross in the year of our Lord sixteen fif–
"

"Young Atkins!" A high-pitched voice shouted from behind me. "I thought that was you over there, boy."

When I turned around to look, I saw a slender figure dressed in a dark hooded cloak and scarf which obscured most of their face.

"Don't tell me you've simply forgotten about our important arrangement today, have ye, boy?" The cloaked figure lorded over the boy, and pointed a gnarled, accusatory finger down at him. "I'm warning you, don't tell me you no longer wish to do the simple task you promised. The one I entrusted only to you."

"Of course not, your wise ladyship. Please forgive me." said Atkins, clasping his hands together. "I did not forget. I was just on my merry way to see you, miss."

Having heard just about enough, I said, "There's no need to get nasty with the boy. I'm Terry Doyle. I'm the man who is carrying this boy's hen for him today. May I kindly ask who you are?"

The hooded figure ignored me.

"What an utterly stupid and hopeless gutter rat bastard of a boy you are, Atkins. How very disappointing." The hooded figure's voice filled with hatred. "I perhaps shouldn't be all that surprised, really. This rat-infested burgh the likes of you call home certainly produces all kinds of worthless rodents like you. Now, then, boy, I gather you will no longer be wanting a full year's supply of toffee, oatcakes and many a shiny gaming dice?"

"Hello, excuse me for butting in again here," I said. "I just wanted you … whoever you are, to know I'm responsible for making this young man late for his duties. I'm from out of town, and when I spotted him running down the road with this hen …"

The hooded figure ignored me once more, still facing the boy, and snapped its gnarled fingers.

Immediately, Atkins straightened and spoke in an emotionless tone, and it seemed he was entranced. "I promise to carry out my destined task immediately, dear kind lady of the dark place," he said flatly.

The hooded woman crouched slightly and brought her concealed face worryingly close to Atkins' wide-eyed and dazed state. Unfortunately for me, it was at that very moment that she flipped over her hood and I recognised her instantly. Aside from the singed blackened cloak, Lillian was the same horrid and ghoulish woman I had picked up outside Central Station just over an hour ago.

"As useless as you are, little boy." She continued. "As much as I want to tear the flesh from your body for what you've done to me." Her long, boney fingers skimmed the side of his cheek. "You have a chance to redeem yourself, and redeem yourself you will. Now, quickly, walk with me."

As I readied myself to follow them, everything and everyone froze around me except Lillian. As if she were breaking character from a play, she turned around and said, "Enjoying my show, Terry Doyle?" She laughed, revealing a row of yellowed, spiky teeth. "The only reason you have been able to interact with anybody here is due to the visual experience of my past. I have conjured a little trip for you. Watching you squirm has been fun, but no more. Watch as the memories of my past unfold. You are lost in the world I have brought you to. The people you have spoken to here are fragments of the very real, lost souls I have taken back on this day."

I stepped back as my mind raced with questions. A memory? Lillian's memory? She must've been hundreds of years old. Was she even human? Was she something else? Why bring me here? It's not like I lived in this time. My stomach twisted thinking I had been taken by some demon and forced to see the transgressions of her past.

Before I could think any further on it, time unfroze and Lillian returned to Atkins, dragging the wee boy by the arm. And from that point on, no one seemed to hear or notice me anymore. Refusing to abandon Atkins, memory or no, I followed them both from behind, keeping my eye on the young boy. Fearing for his life … and my own.

Six

Near the end of Vennel, Lillian and Atkins stopped outside a large tenement house away from any prying eyes aside from my own.

"You know Master Hamilton's house up the road," said Lillian, a fierce eagerness in her voice. "Don't you? Don't you?"

"Yes, miss. I know the house well. Some of my family used to be acquainted with—"

"Never mind your pointless nonsense, boy, and listen up. In a moment, I'm going to give you something very special to carry over to Mr Hamilton's house. You must be very careful not to drop this on your way over there. Do you understand, Atkins?"

The boy nodded in agreement.

Lillian reached into her cloak and fished out a decorative navy-blue glass bottle, about half a litre in size. "Now, young man, this here is a very fragile tincture indeed. Very shortly, my boy, you will be the carrier of a great flame concealed within."

At this point, Atkins' eyes widened, and he moved closer to the bottle, drawn to it like a moth to light. "Are you telling me that'll be bottled fire you're trusting me to carry, miss? I'll carry a great flame?"

"Oh, if you believe that, wee guy, you'll believe anything," I said, getting closer to him. "Now, listen to me, you could hear me fine ten minutes ago. Come back away from that mad woman, son. She's no good. She's dangerous."

Once again, it appeared no one could see or hear me, and I soon came to realise that what I was witnessing here was what Lillian wanted me to see. A dark dramatic sequence for me to observe. A memory of hers.

"Today we stand at Glasgow Cross in the year of our Lord sixteen fif–" the boy had said just before Lillian intervened. I was witnessing a memory, folks, Glasgow Cross in the year sixteen fifty-something, and now I had to find out why.

Atkins slowly reached for the bottle. "I'm to carry magic fire? Like Merlin? Like the wizard Marina told me about."

"Don't mention her name, you gutter rat," Lillian snapped, her eyes burning with rage. She raised her fingers towards his throat to choke him, but quickly pulled away and continued. "Yes, my wee Glaswegian dear, it is full of magical fire and much more," she said, pinching his cheek like an adoring mother or aunty might do.

The boy's eyes remained fascinated by the bottle.

"How about one last treat from me before I entrust this into your caring hands?" Lillian withdrew the bottle back again from the boy's longing grasp.

"Is it some more magic?" he asked with a slowly widening smile.

"Of course it is. It is somewhat of a parting gift for now. I am going to light up the inside of this very bottle nice and pretty for you — like the moon and the stars in the night's sky. My mystical bottle will light the way for you. One little tap from my finger on its neck here should do the trick."

As soon as Lillian tapped the bottle, a mysterious power awakened within it. Strands of light pulsated, then, as if flicking on a lightbulb, the bottle beamed to life. I honestly couldn't believe what I was seeing. The light burst from the glass vessel and illuminated the entire archway. That's when I noticed three rather well-fed rats scurrying past my feet in fear of it.

Lillian smirked and offered the bottle to Atkins. The boy, trapped under some spell, eagerly grasped his tiny hands around it and nodded to her in a creepy sort of reverence. His eyes widened and he stared into it utterly mystified, like a toddler exploring a Christmas snow globe for the first time. He began walking towards the Hamilton House as the fire within the bottle swirled and dimmed, mutating into a fiery shade of amber.

"Walk on and fulfil your task, Atkins," said Lillian, her once honeyed words turned venomous. "By tonight you will have made Glaswegian history, my boy. Giving the despots of this city a piece of what has been taken from me. What you, dear boy, have taken from me."

As the boy walked on, I followed, but not before turning back once to notice Lillian's gleeful pale face smiling back at me. She really was enjoying watching me go through all of this, she was relishing it.

"I know who you are," I shouted at Lillian. "If anything happens to that wee boy, I swear I'll come looking for you, and you can guarantee I won't stop until one of us is dead."

Her venomous face lingered on Atkins for a moment, then faded back into the darkness of the alleyway. After she vanished, I tried to catch up with Atkins, to hopefully put a stop to whatever she had tricked him into doing.

Off in the distance, I recognised the boy's silhouette hurrying toward the Hamilton House. I shouted his name and wondered whether he heard me now Lillian had vanished. "Atkins! Hold on just a second, son, will ye? The deal you just made, I'll offer you a better one, just please don't do whatever she's told you."

The boy remained unflinching, his eyes fixed on the house as the bottle pulsed a violent red. Between the running and shouting, I quickly lost my breath. My pace slowed and I helplessly watched Atkins distance himself further from me. "Atkins," I said, then paused for a quick breath. "Look, ye have to try and listen to me, son."

The boy walked onwards, gazing feverishly into the bottle. Whatever was inside had now begun to bubble as tendrils of smoke rose from Atkins' hands, burning a bright red. Soon, a strong smell of singed skin came towards me. The boy remained unflinching and carried on seemingly pain-free. Lillian's trance dug deep within him, and I wondered if he was screaming on the inside and no one could hear.

What was certain, though, was that I had been brought here by this demon to see all of this happen. I felt completely and utterly helpless as I witnessed these events from a Scrooge-like perspective, facing the ghosts of times long past. Finally accepting my role in this twisted world, I did the only thing I could do and prayed for the wee boy's soul as I watched him approach a big iron gate that was half open.

As I followed him behind this gate, I soon realised I had seen this very courtyard before. This was the place I had seen the girl with the wicker basket walk towards, wishing to deliver her master's cleaned belt buckles. Past the courtyard, Atkins headed towards a barnhouse which had iron grated windows and resembled more of a workhouse. In the middle of the courtyard there was a large well, and several soaked garments lying stacked up on a wooden wheelbarrow right next to it. Atkins, who was still in a trance and carrying whatever brewed-up misery that witch of a woman had placed in the bottle, had now come to a stop at the red-painted wooden door of the barn-type building. An engraved plaque above the door read:

Residence of J. Hamilton
6 North Vennel Way

Atkins stared mindlessly up at the plaque and slowly took his left hand off the bottle — the contents of which were still bubbling and spitting what looked like embers. Atkins, grasping only the neck of the bottle, cocked his arm back behind his shoulder and readied himself to toss it.

"Come on, pal, isn't that taking chap door runaway to the extreme?"

Atkins flung the bottle from his hand, and it shattered off the Hamilton residence as if lighting had struck against their door.

Before any of you all go thinking along the lines of the classic Molotov cocktail here, you are a long way off. It appeared to me that whatever chemically dreadful concoction Lillian had put inside the bottle did not even require any igniting. Once it had struck the door, it exploded like nothing from the natural world. Within seconds, the flames had risen from nowhere, quickly spreading over the roof and engulfing the Hamilton estate.

As this unholy fire melted stone and brick, it spread dangerously close to Atkins. As if it was a cruel joke, the boy snapped out of his trance just before the flames swallowed the poor soul.

The last thing I remember is the skin of his face melting away.

Seven

After seeing what happened to Atkins, I didn't notice I had been running until I fell over and tumbled to the ground. Quickly recovering, I realised I had tripped over that wooden wheelbarrow near the well. From behind, the heat from the flames was so suffocating I considered throwing myself into the well. Thankfully, though, whatever fragments were still left of my mostly lost mind had decided to act sensibly and fight my instincts, and so I kept running.

The most daunting thing was not really knowing where to run, where I could find safety in not just a place that I didn't know, but a whole different time I didn't belong in. Even when I tried to stop running for a couple of seconds to look over my shoulder, all I saw were those hellish flames sweeping their way over wooden houses and screaming people. The next building ahead of me was this little chapel house, standing on a steep hill with a pathway leading up to an arched doorway.

Thinking of no better option, I proceeded up the hill. When I reached the top, my sluggish and tired legs gave in and soon I was on the ground once again. Although I do remember thanking God for getting me out of harm's way before collapsing.

Unluckily for me, though, I turned and glanced down the hill and at the malevolent blaze spreading closer to me. Realising every precious second couldn't be wasted, I rolled over on my side and noticed the chapel house itself was a few feet away.

I mustered any remaining energy left in my legs and crawled towards the chapel's doorway. Above the door, a metallic plaque possessed an engraving and, at that moment, I felt like I had lost my mind all over again:

BEYOND THIS DOOR LIES
THE CITY OF GLASGOW
2019
POPULATION 611,748

I simply lay on the hill and closed my eyes to pray to God for help once again.

May you forgive me, Lord, but if my fate right now is to lie in some coma, can ye at least change it to a deep sleep not full of waking nightmares, for fuck's sake.

Suddenly, my rapid chain of overthinking stopped. The chapel doors flew open as if someone had kicked them. I froze in panic, believing it was all over, and that the demon Lillian was about to emerge from that chapel for a final showdown. I lay waiting for the death that she would no doubt bring to me, but as the seconds turned into minutes and the screams from the burning inhabitants of the old city at the bottom of the hill grew louder, nobody emerged from the chapel doorway.

I decided to take a chance. Those church doors would either lead me down to another, deeper layer of the hell that Lillian had created for me, or they would take me back to reality and out of this nightmare. What else did I have to lose at that point?

I steadied myself back onto my feet and headed for the doors. Before going through them, I took one last look back down the hill.

Now, ten years later to this very day, I swear on my miserable life to you all that what I saw from that hilltop was like staring into a vision of Hell from the minds of painters such as Hieronymus Bosch. Far and wide I helplessly watched men, women, and young children scream in agony as they were being roasted alive. No one in the town could flee such horror, as whole sections had been decimated in mere minutes. As I stared in abhorrence at the God-awful bonfire being stoked with flesh and bone, the face of that vile demon, Lillian, emerged right out of the smoke and grinned.

Feeling powerless and alone, I couldn't stand to face any more of the trickery and malice fiercely spreading throughout that place. I turned and limped my way through the arched doorway of the chapel and into darkness.

After slowly walking a few steps, the ground crumbled beneath me, and I fell quickly into the abyss. It was just like those dreams we have of falling from a great height, although we wake up right before hitting the ground. However, I did not wake up. The ground I slammed onto was the cold, rain-swept cobblestones of Cathedral Precinct. When I opened my eyes, I was facing the James Lumsden statue and my taxi parked just ahead.

Intermission One

After having mustered the courage and energy he had left to tell his fellow churchgoers the truth, Terry watched disappointingly the doubtful faces of his auld friends inside the church.

"Now, I can tell by the looks on your faces that you believe none of what I have just told you. I would like to say just how shallow I think it is for a Christian community who believes in so much to refuse to believe an evil has and still is torturing a man who thought himself a true friend to you."

The audience made no reply and instead looked on with even bigger looks of scepticism.

"My story isn't done yet," Terry continued. "Please, folks, an evil is coming, and I fear something bad may happen to you all. This evil does not spare the innocent. You must be informed of what's coming." Terry sighed, overwhelmed with the image of Glasgow burning. "I won't ask you to stay. So please, feel free to leave not just here, but Glasgow, if you don't want to bear the shock of seeing for yourselves this very real evil incarnate."

"Aye, the shock of you boring us all to death with this fantasy story, Doyle. You're an absolute disgrace to our church with your paranormal satanic talk. Go back to wherever the hell ye were hiding," said auld Jim Clarke, who used to be bad with the gambling through his youth and adulthood. At the age of sixty-two, he decided to ask God for help with his card and dice problem, and the Lord helped him. Now, at seventy-two, he was probably the holiest and grumpiest auld fella in Pastor Hugh's born-again community.

"That's quite a lot of mentions of Satan, the paranormal, and Hell, Jim," said Hugh, standing up from his seat. "Especially for a man who supposedly claims he is spiritually reborn. Now, button it and stop shouting out of turn in my church." Hugh pointed at Jim from the altar and the auld man kept silent. "I believe the main thing that we are failing to grasp here, people, is that Terry came back to us. After all that time, he has come back. He is not looking for fame, or money, or even sympathy. He is back to tell his story and he clearly needs our help with something, don't ye, Terry?"

"That's right, Hugh, but I want them to know that they may leave right now if they want to avoid the very demonic thing I met that night."

Hugh rubbed the sides of his head, relieving the mounting headache coming before him. "Terry, could I have a quick wee word with ye?

Terry nodded and followed Hugh to the side of the altar away from the audience.

"Thanks for believing me, Hugh. Let me tell you more of what happened. I'll convince them, like I did you."

Hugh sighed. "In all fairness, Terry, I couldn't tell you in front of all these people, but I personally don't believe your story one bit, my friend."

"That's ok for now, Hugh. You'll see, like the rest of them. May God will you into seeing this pressing evil."

"Excuse me, Hugh," said a gentle-sounding voice from behind Terry. "Am I still to bring the hymn books round today, love, or are you doing something a wee bit different this morning?"

"Don't know if we'll have time this Sunday, Delilah," said Pastor Hugh. The sweetly-smiling older lady had short, silvery hair and possessed a set of deep blue eyes which hinted at her having been a beautiful woman in years past. She wore a bright pink cardigan and a pair of black non-slip shoes. Pastor Hugh had come to know this woman as the grandmotherly, kind and God-abiding Delilah Duncan.

Delilah sighed, then said, in a soft and endearing tone, "Well, that's a wee shame. You'll have to wait until next Sunday to see the repair work I've done on those tattered auld hymn books."

Hugh smirked. "I heard you had some plans for those badly neglected songbooks of ours. Well, we love how you're always creative with your spare time for the good of others, Delilah."

"It's nae bother. I like to do my bit for the church. I might be showing my age these days, but I still know a thing or two about breathing some new life into these things."

"Could ye try breathing some of that life into me, please, dear?" Terry asked Delilah in a cheerful tone. "You've been listening to my strange but true story, you can perhaps tell I'm in desperate need of your kind of energy and spirit."

"I am sure the good Lord has much more to offer you than me, pet. May he bless you for telling your story here today."

"Thank you, that's really kind of you to say. I hope the others will see it the same way."

"Don't mention it, son," Delilah said with a wink, which seemed a bit strange, though Terry quickly found it to be reassuring. "I will be here to listen to the rest of your story to the end, son." Delilah gestured toward Hugh. "And so will your good friend and pastor here."

"Aye, I certainly will," said Hugh. "Terry has been very brave telling us his story today. Although I can sadly see Mr Clarke, his granddaughters, and the McCormick family now making their way to the door." Hugh waved and shouted, "Enjoy the rest of your Sunday, folks. Hopefully we'll see you back next week."

The church door slammed, and Delilah turned back to Terry. "Well, I think I'll go have a wee seat and prepare to hear the rest of this story," she said, winking at Terry once more.

"Feel free to rest your legs for a bit, Delilah." Hugh said. "The new tea and coffee machine is just over there. We got a good deal with the Fairtrade Company. It's only a pound a cup." He snapped his fingers as if an idea came to mind. "I nearly forgot to ask, how's your Tommy doing, are the new inhalers helping him?"

"Tommy …" Delilah's voice drifted, and a puzzled look crossed her face.

"Your husband Tommy, of course. I remember you telling me just the other week his asthma has been a bit tougher this time of year, and he has had to get a stronger steroid inhaler."

"Oh yes, aye, my Tommy," Delilah said, "He's doing a lot better now with the new meds."

"Well, that's good to hear, be sure to bring him along on a Sunday if he's well enough, we would love to meet him."

"He would love to meet all of you as well. Right, I think I will go for a wee cup of tea after all, see you in a bit, then," Delilah said, turning and walking in the direction of where the folks who had stayed to hear more of Terry's story were seated.

Despite some of the churchgoers leaving and most of the remainder seeming doubtful and unsure of Terry, he appreciated the people who kindly decided to stay and hear him out. Sitting on a church's bench in the front row was Jesse Rhodes, knitting a scarf with an uncanny precision and speed. She always knitted in church on a Sunday. Behind Jesse was the Bell family, who ran the Coral Reef chip shop in the city. Glen and Maureen Bell had joined the Millers Park Christian Hall community just a couple of months before Terry Doyle had vanished. Terry always remembered them as caring, hard-working people, and since then it seemed they had had twin daughters no older than nine that were with them today.

It was pleasantly reassuring but slightly emotional for him to see his old neighbours, Teresa and James Dickson, remain seated to hear the rest of his story. When Terry smiled at them appreciatively from the altar, both returned heartfelt glances, as if he had their support. Just to the left were another two families he didn't recognise. They were a sort of hippy-looking couple in their late forties. Both possessed dangling long hair and wore flowery, oversized shirts, which appeared to embarrass their teenage son sitting cross-armed next to them.

"I can see your followers have certainly grown in numbers since I've been gone, Hugh."

"Aye, they have indeed. I like to think of them as my family," said Hugh, his eyes heavy with happiness and pride.

"Well, as you can see, some of them decided to up and leave because of me, I'm sorry for that."

"Don't pay them any mind, I think you and me both expected that might happen anyway. Maybe some stories are just too out of the ordinary for some people of our faith, Terry. Some of them just want to say their prayers at night, agree the Lord saves all and go to bed and forget about it."

Terry pondered Hugh's words for a moment and glanced across the remaining crowd. "And what about the ones who've stayed?"

"They still might not believe what happened to you, but perhaps they'll be willing to see if God is hidden in the details as well as the demons."

"God appears nowhere in my story, Hugh, nor was I able to ever really find him in my heart again. That's part of the reason I'm here today. It's been a long, dark road."

"That may be, but I've always believed God takes his time when working through people. Perhaps you must tell your story in its entirety before reconnecting with Him. What I can clearly see, though, is that you're feeling a lot better after speaking for just an hour."

"Aye, I do. It's been a heavy weight to carry. Living alone with nothing but my thoughts … I'm just thankful for the patience of the people who've stayed on, especially those who don't even know me." Terry cocked his head toward the older woman hunched over sipping her tea. "Like that Delilah. She's pleasant to talk with."

"She is. Recently, the poor soul does all she can for her husband. Has been giving up most of her time on Sundays to come here. On some Thursdays she does the nightly bible study group, where she reads to the younger ones."

Terry lowered his head, thinking of Shauna. "I hope her husband pulls through."

"I believe he will. You know, as much as I believe in the Almighty, behind every great man there is a great woman. Speaking of those great women, here comes my saviour now." Hugh said, a smile creasing his mouth.

Terry turned to see Gloria McClelland for the first time in ten years. She came walking down the church aisle towards them, wearing a long, dark blue winter coat. She had long, straightened dark brown hair dangling down her back, and it suited her. She had always been a glamorous-looking woman, but was also modest, cheerful, and, more importantly, down to earth. Just the very presence of Hugh's wife caught the attention of everyone, with some folks even standing up to make themselves be seen and heard saying good afternoon to her.

"Hello and good afternoon, brothers and sisters, how are you all today?" Gloria said to them as she passed by. She walked up the two steps onto the church's altar where Hugh and Terry stood and hugged Terry immediately.

"My goodness, Terry Doyle," Gloria grinned, revealing a row of sparkling teeth, which after a few moments hid again behind a worrying frown. She softly smacked Terry on the shoulder. "Don't put us through anything like that again." Her voice cracked as she hugged him.

"That's why I am here today, Gloria. I'm telling them all the truth of what happened that night. Things they need to hear. I'm really trying and–"

"I know. Some of them have even been so rude as to leave. Must think it's a made-up fantasy."

Terry dipped his head, knowing his story sounded strange. As with Hugh, he wanted Gloria to believe him. "What do you think?"

Gloria paused before speaking. "Hugh has been texting me some key parts."

"Sorry for not telling you," Hugh said. "I hope you don't mind. Gloria had to drop the kids at her ma's, and I wanted to fill her in on the basics."

"It's alright, Hugh," Terry looked towards Gloria. "So, you know something demonic began hunting me, then?"

"It's not the sanest story," said Gloria. "But if you believe it, Terry, so do I. I have always thought that if there is a Holy Spirit, then there must be the possibility of unholy spirits and dark entities in our world too."

Gloria looked as if she wanted to say more, but paused.

"What is it?" asked Terry.

"You know I hate to tell ye, but I have some bad news."

"It's fine, Gloria, just hit me with it."

"We tried to get back in touch with Anne but I'm afraid—"

"Christ, no …" Terry began saying as he swept his hands over his head. In his mind he was seeing all his worst fears coming to life for his wife and son. It was her; Lillian's lifeless eyes and pale face smiling devilishly in his mind. She had got his wife and son because she knew he had come back to Glasgow. She knew his real reason for coming back … to stop her.

"No, Terry. Hold on. You're getting ahead of yourself. Anne and your boy are both safe and well."

Terry sighed as if a weight crushing his heart had been lifted.

"Although," Gloria continued. "Her and David are living in Carlisle now."

"I thought she would move on from here anyway." Terry looked around the church, remembering their time together. "Too many memories."

"They've got better over the years," Gloria said, trying to sound cheerful. "Anne's got a steady job and David's at university there."

"You've kept in touch, then, aye?"

"After a while we didn't want Anne to feel like we were calling her all the time to drag up the past. We kept in touch for the most part, talked about David and work, trying to avoid your name, which would just upset her. After the polis stopped looking, the calls dwindled and then eventually stopped altogether and …"

"What my Gloria is trying to tell ye here, Terry," Hugh interjected. "Is that time moves on and eventually so do people. Anne waited a long time, but she couldn't wait forever. She needed to grieve and find a new way forward. The fact is, she waited as long as she could."

From the look on Gloria's face, Hugh's bluntness was something she had tried to avoid. "That's right, as I was going to say. Although my husband could refrain from interrupting me."

Hugh nodded, as if him interrupting her like this had happened before. "Forgive me, my queen, you're the boss."

"So she doesn't want to see me, then?" asked Terry, his voice cracking.

"I spoke with her this morning, just over an hour ago, in fact, but she …"

"She doesn't want to know me anymore." Terry sighed, feeling the weight of losing his family over again. "I guess with all the worry I put them through I can't say I blame her, Gloria."

"I'm sorry," said Gloria. "Give her some time, she'll come around. There is some good news, though."

"Aye, and what's that?"

"Just before I got off the phone, I managed to ask her if she would be letting David know you're back."

"And?" Terry asked in a slightly desperate tone.

"She said you're still David's dad and, of course, he has a right to know. He's an adult now. She said it's up to him if he wants to reconnect and that she'll keep a hold of our number to pass on. Before we ended the call she said she's not sure how he'll react."

Terry felt a sinking feeling in his stomach. "I never wanted to leave. I had to … it wasn't a choice." Terry gazed darkly at the statue near the altar.

Hugh wrapped his arm around his auld friend. "Just give it time. It'll take a wee while, but you'll get back to where you want to be."

"Aye, I hope so."

"Well," said Hugh. "I think it's high time this good man here gets to the rest of his story."

"Right, let's get the rest of this done and over with," Terry agreed as the three of them parted ways for now.

"Wait, Hugh. One last thing before I start again." Terry said in a much lower tone of voice.

"Aye, what is it?"

"Listen, right behind that statue of our Lord on the cross over there I planked something away before I disappeared."

"Sorry, say that again, you did what?

"I hid something behind it ten years ago, and it should still be there today."

"Well … what the heck was it that you had to hide in the Lord's church?" Hugh asked with a puzzled look.

"It's something that's sought after by the very demon that haunted me that night. It's part of the reason I came. When you've listened to the next part of my story you'll understand. For now, though, just try and keep it between us."

"Eh … aye, alright then, I suppose. I'm just hoping you haven't gone and lost the plot on me already, have you?"

"Nah, I haven't lost it just yet. Just you go over and join Gloria, but don't tell her for the time being. I'll call you both over to speak to you when I'm done. By that time you'll know what's hidden there."

"Okay, then, if it's something that's going to help you," Hugh said somewhat hesitantly. "Anyway, me and Gloria are with ye all the way, whatever help you need, Terry."

Hugh turned, leaving Terry alone at the altar with the microphone stand, and sat down next to his wife and Delilah Duncan. Before Terry resumed his story, he felt tempted to whisper into Gloria's ear what Terry had said about the Christ statue and fought that temptation for his best pal's sake. He did, however, glance quickly at the statue of Jesus on the cross, which stood overlooking the altar, then at Terry readying himself by the microphone.

What could he have hidden behind that cross statue? Hugh thought. *Whatever it is, it's been here the whole time Terry was gone? Why did he need it? And why does this so-called demon want it?* When thinking this over in his mind, Pastor Hugh felt a chill work its way through him.

"Okay, folks," said Terry over the mic. "Let's get to where I left off earlier." He inhaled a deep breath. "Right, I had been in a memory of the seventeenth century where I had been taken by Lillian and then finding myself back in the present-day Glasgow I knew and lived in ..."

PART IV

The Legend of John Dunlop and the Realm Daemoniorum Book

Eight

After walking through the chapel doors and falling, I ended up lying on the cold, hard ground staring into the night. I leaned forward, rubbing my back, and noticed the Gothic tower of Glasgow Cathedral piercing upward into the sky. As I slowly eased onto my feet, nothing felt broken, which seemed like a miracle given the night's events, and I realised I had been lying right in the middle of Cathedral Precinct.

Even though the west door was most likely locked at that hour, I moved closer to the cathedral, standing in the warm glow of those lights illuminating the eight-hundred-and-twenty-four-year-old house of God. Sheltering under the front archway, I wrung out, as best I could, my Harrington coat, and felt a strange sense of déjà vu about the cathedral. I mean, even to this day, I'm almost certain I had seen a much earlier and newer-looking version back where Lillian had taken me, but it still felt odd.

As I stood there, wrapping my arms together and shivering, I still had no idea what this Lillian woman wanted with me. Why had she chosen to show me that part of the past? Why did she want me to see that memory of hers? What did I have to do with any of it? I was a cabbie driver with little money and little to offer.

Unable to answer the questions burning inside my mind, I decided I needed to simply get moving again, if only to warm me up a bit. Walking from the entrance, I noticed my taxicab sitting just a short distance away on Cathedral Street, and my hopes lifted for a moment, imagining the heater blasting on my hands and face. As I quickly made my way back to it, I noticed the passenger door had been opened. For a moment, I feared that, once I got inside, I would be taken yet again through some other time portal where Lillian would be waiting. Honestly, for all I knew, I could have been entering a cab full of Lovecraftian creatures yanking me to the depths of wherever this demonic enchantress dwelled. After that night, nothing seemed impossible. My hands started shaking and, for whatever reason, whether it was fear or something else, I could not drive the taxi. I decided to leave it there and call Hugh to come pick me up.

I assumed Hugh would've questions, seeing my cab within arm's length, and I realised telling a story like this to either Hugh, my family, or the polis would land me in the lovely padded room of the priory asylum. I decided it would be best for now not to tell Hugh or the rest of the family what had happened to me just yet. All I would tell them was that somebody had given me a bit of a scare, and I had some trouble with a looney passenger. It had happened before, hopefully it would be believable enough. These were the lies I was going to tell my nearest and dearest friends and family. It took me ten years to the day to finally tell you the whole truth. For my sake and yours.

I knew my phone was where I always kept it, in my cab's wee storage container, on the driver's side of the taxi just beneath the door handle. As I reached closer to it, I suddenly heard a very familiar voice. It wasn't cold and cruel like Lillian's, but a voice I hadn't heard in a heartbreakingly long year — a voice a grieving parent desperately yearned to hear once more.

"Gotcha again, Dad. Two, nil," said the soft and sweet voice in a playful manner.

I turned around, my heart beating faster, eager to see my little girl. But there was nobody to be seen.

"Got you yet again, Pops, you're too slow. Try turning the other way."

Immediately, I whipped back around to face my taxi.

The driver's side door slammed shut. I reached for the handle to pull it ajar again, finding a strong force resisting me, when a tiny pale hand appeared on the driver's side window. Her little fingers tapped the glass, ever so lightly, and I finally saw my deceased daughter again.

She was dressed in the same light-blue hospital gown she had worn when she slipped away. Her cheeks were a rosy pink and her shiny blonde hair dangled down to her shoulders. Tears welled in my eyes as I admired her beautiful face filled with life.

"A kind lady brought me back to see you again, Dad. You happy to see me?" she asked.

I opened my mouth to speak, but said nothing, overwhelmed at seeing her again. I felt my mouth stretch into the biggest smile I could manage, and I nodded silently.

"For a while, I felt I was swimming in an endless sea of dark water," Shauna said, her eyes drifting past me. "But a nice lady found me and brought me back. She says she is here to help us, to reunite us again. Are Mum and David going to be here soon?"

So there she was, my dearly departed wee girl talking to me from inside my cab's passenger window. My Shauna looked nothing like she did when I held her hand as she released her last breath. She looked healthy and strong. She looked like everything I wanted for her and more. The pain of knowing she had been denied a long life raced through me. My tears came quickly, releasing some of the guilt and grief which had consumed me for the last year.

"Come with me to meet her, Dad. She is waiting in the City of the Dead, just up the hill from here."

The taxi's passenger door swung open and the petite, ethereal figure of my daughter stepped out. She reached for my hand and her icy touch coursed like poison through my bones. As strong as my love still was for the many memories of my little girl, a feeling of alarm caused me to back away from her. Something wasn't right.

"Aren't you pleased I'm back?" she asked me belatedly with a sulking voice.

"Shauna," I said, running my hands through my head. "Can ye just stop a minute?"

"Stop what, Dad? Don't you want to hug me?"

"Please, sweetheart. Give Dad a wee minute to clear his head and think."

Shauna stomped her small, bare feet on the rain-soaked concrete of Cathedral Street and the ground trembled.

A temper tantrum? The Shauna I knew never pulled a hissy fit for anything.

"Darling, just be careful. You'll end up breaking all your wee toes doing that."

"Just take my hand," she demanded. "I'll guide you to the nice lady. She's waiting, let's go."

"Shauna, just hear me out a second, will ye? We really can't trust who I think you are talking about, darlin."

"But why, Dad?"

"Because she's the one who's been causing all this mayhem tonight."

"No, she bloody well hasn't. Why are you being so mean, Dad? You need to come with me now."

"Shauna, she's not here to help us, darlin."

Her face turned a bright red and she screamed the loudest I had ever heard her. Clenching her fists on either side of her, she said, "You've had your chance. You, Mum and David, enjoy the rest of your lives. I'm off to visit Lady Lillian, who will bring me back forever and will help me find a nice family."

The next thing I knew, my daughter dashed away from me past the statue of James White. As bizarre and macabre as my entire situation had been that night, I wouldn't be able to live with myself if I didn't pursue her. I couldn't let her slip away … not again.

"Please, stop running, Shauna. Come back a minute. I've changed my mind. I'll come. Wait for me to catch up, will ye? We can go up to the auld boneyard together."

As I hurried after her, she pushed open a large black-and-gold-painted gate and I watched as the white fabric of Shauna's nightgown slowly faded from view. It was just as though I had lost her all over again.

Nine

I decided to continue in the direction in which my wee girl had vanished. If she was heading to the necropolis as she had told me, then I would be able to reach her there soon. It was time for me to seek answers about this crazy night. More importantly, I needed to find out just what kind of supernatural force Lillian was and why she had brought my family into it. Was she a ghost? A demon? Or some type of malevolent spirit I had somehow unintentionally angered?

When hurrying further on, I crossed this auld, well-known bridge, the Bridge of Sighs. I leaned over and watched the traffic passing below. In that moment, I wished for nothing more than to be in one of those cars, driving as far away as I could from this long and dead part of the city.

Past the bridge, I arrived at two winding paths in either direction. The right one led up to a higher slope of the hill, where there was yet another long winding row of moss-covered and ancient tombstones. In the centre of these forking paths, where the terrain was hilly with some old crumbling steps, stood a unique monument built in the form of an arched doorway. As hard as it was to see in the gloom of the dead of night, however, I discerned some of what the inscription read:

**THE ADJOINING BRIDGE
WAS ERECTED BY
THE MERCHANTS HOUSE OF GLASGOW**

The rest of the inscription was faded and barely visible in the dark, but I deciphered a rather uplifting quote at the bottom, which the remainder of you today will appreciate:

"BLESSED IS THE MAN WHO TRUSTETH IN GOD
AND WHOSE HOPE THE LORD IS"

I read the quote once more and felt like it was God's way of telling me not to give up.

After several minutes, I reached the second-highest summit of the Glasgow Necropolis and stopped to catch my breath, admiring the many headstones and mausoleums layered within our history. Off in the distance, I noticed a decrepit vardo wagon, which resembled something from the days of Dick Turpin. As the wagon turned along the gravel past a few headstones, its wheels moaned, as if carrying the torturous sounds of the dead. In the faint hues of night, its blackened paint emanated a sickly green, revealing on the side intricately carved patterns amid golden lettering, which read:

AD ITER MEDICINA
SPECTACULUM

Perhaps a couple of hundred years ago this thing may not have looked out of the ordinary, but I couldn't remember seeing any coaches or buckboards on those seventeenth-century streets Lillian had transported me to. At that point, I assumed she was inside the moving wagon, maybe even on her way to possess the resting souls of the cemetery. A dark thought sprang up in my mind. Maybe she had already taken possession of my deceased daughter's soul? Was that even

Shauna, or some trick of the mind? I clenched my fist, wanting to know what kind of hell Lillian had brought on my family and me.

"Here, coach driver!" I shouted, attempting to sound confident. "Or whoever is inside this shabby antique. Stop and come out, will ye?"

Ignoring me, the wagon continued.

Eventually, I caught up to the front of the vardo, only to see nobody driving the carriage. The sound of horse hooves struck the narrow concrete path. Then came into view the spectral silhouette of a very strong Hackney horse. Its long and fierce face possessed a pair of burning red eyes alive with molten flame, as if reflecting the fiery pits of Hell.

Immediately, I retreated from the horse and smacked my hand against the wagon, beckoning its owner to come forth. "Lillian! Or whatever you liked to be called. I know you're in there. What in Christ's name did you do to my Shauna? Come out and tell me. You've sent me on this rollercoaster ride. Tell me, for God's sake, what for? Why all this madness?"

A few seconds passed and the corporeal horse halted in front of an old, overgrown dike covered in moss with an isolated, sagging tree. Trying to get a better look, I crept past the deathly horse staring at me with its fiery eyes and noticed the shadowy silhouette of a body dangling from one of the tree's branches. The person was small, a child, presumably, and reeked of death. My heart sank; the child dangling on the rope appeared to be around my Shauna's age.

Sorry for using the Lord's name in vain here, but Jesus Christ, what I saw was awful. Only a monster not of this world would harm a child like this. I soon fell to my knees, thinking my wee girl swung gently from the branch above me.

"Very interesting, Mr Doyle, how you find mine and your deceased kin so alike," said a cold and familiar voice from behind.

I sprang to my feet and turned to face her.

Ten

Standing only a foot away from me, Lillian appeared a little different from the time of Glasgow's Great Fire. Her complexion was deathly pale, while her eyes resembled soulless, blackened pits. She was no longer dressed in a black mediaeval-style cloak, but in a long, crimson leather trench coat. She wore a dark wide-brimmed hat that made her look like a cross between a witch and a dangerous-seeming biker, and her hair hung past her shoulders and appeared dark with sporadic streaks of silver running through it.

"You have been a very good boy tonight, Apostol," Lillian said to the ghostly stallion who had been pulling the wagon. "Unfortunately," she brushed the horse's sickly green mane. "Horses who've been dead for nearly four hundred years can't properly eat their favourite clumps of sugar like they used to, can they, sweetie?" The horse whinnied in agreement, then Lillian turned towards me. "Right, Terry, where were we?"

"Where were we?" I said, enraged, and stepped towards her with both of my fists clenched. "How about we start with why you have been torturing me since I picked you up at the station? Or why you lured me up here to show me an image of my child hanging from the tree?" I said, pointing towards the branch.

Lillian did not utter a word, but simply shook her head as though I was in the wrong about something.

"Didn't you hear, Terry Doyle, what I said about my kin and yours being alike? Look once more. The sweet girl swinging from that tree is not your daughter, but mine," she said, her voice exposing a hint of humanity. "Better yet, let me show you how our paths align." Lillian flicked her spindly hand into the air and muttered under her breath. A fierce, fiery glow appeared around her, and the next thing I knew, everything around me was spinning.

The old headstones and cathedral started to whirl like a wicked carousel from which there was no departure. The only thing not turning was Lillian. Those dark bottomless pits she had for eyes stayed fixed on me. Just as I was on the verge of passing out, she raised her left hand into the air and lowered it again slowly as if she were a puppeteer and I the puppet.

Everything had stopped spinning and, for the moment, seemed to be back to normal. I found myself standing at the top of a rocky hill, staring at miles and miles of countryside. The light piercing through the clouds indicated it was morning, and the dreary night sky once above me had been replaced with a pleasant, sunny day. Above me, hawks circled around the naked, rocky terrain. A gentle breeze glided across my face and the air felt crisp and refreshing. I inhaled a deep breath when I heard the ringing of church bells tolling not too far in the distance.

"Where or wit point in time have you dragged me to now?" I asked.

Appearing next to me, Lillian answered. "You're standing in the very same location you were at only a minute ago. However, this time you are inside another memory of mine, well over three hundred and fifty years ago, in fact."

"Why? What do your memories have to do with me?"

"In due course, Terrance Doyle. In due course," she said, then cunningly smirked.

I sighed, knowing I had no choice but to observe whatever she wanted me to see. "So what year is this memory now?" I asked with a tad of desperation in my voice. I wanted this sped up and over with.

"You do not need to know all of the whats and whys. You have already relived one of my most cherished memories of this revoltingly-tainted burgh you nowadays call home."

"The fire of Glasgow? Aye, I experienced your so-called cherished memory alright. Sending an innocent wee boy to his death in those horrific flames?"

"Oh no," Lillian said, holding up her finger. "That wee boy you claim was innocent was simply a means to an end. Revenge. A mother's revenge for her daughter. That day of the Great Fire I made Glasgow pay for what they did to me and my Marina," she said, bowing her head as though in mourning. In the daylight, Lillian looked different, like a feeble, grey-haired shell of a woman that had lost her mind long ago. I realised then that, whatever kind of powerful demonic entity she was now, at one point she had been human — even a mother.

"I'm sorry you lost her," I said, remembering Shauna. "As you are aware, I too know what it's like losing a child."

"My Marina was all I had ... and those dogs took her from me, much like that disease took your child. Watch and understand, Terry Doyle."

Shifting my gaze from Lillian, I saw the same tree from the necropolis in my time, albeit livelier. From below, crowds of people arrived, donned in Celtic-patterned shirts of saffron and emerald. Burly men with unruly beards and hilted swords led the mob chanting in dialects which seemed familiar to me.

Behind them, most of the women wore long dresses with unique and different tartan-styled shawls and linen head cloths, clasping their hands together and bowing in prayer while the younger ladies appeared to be dressed in a similar fashion to milkmaids. I soon realised I stood amongst the townsfolk of Glasgow during the seventeenth century.

"May the demon and her spawn suffer a thousand hells," shouted an elderly woman, angrily throwing her straw hat onto the ground. "A thousand curses upon you."

Most of the crowd then cheered in support, thrusting their arms viciously towards the sky.

Near the front of the crowd was a butch man with long red hair dressed in tattered blue clothes, cheering. In between barbaric shouting, he savagely bit the leg of lamb he held tightly in his hand as meat dribbled down his chin. He smiled with a mouth full of food at a young dark-haired woman in a green dress. The young woman held out a wicker basket filled with apples and berries and was selling them out to the crowd as if it was a football match.

I navigated through the crowd with ease, since, just as before, nobody could see or hear me. I was finding my situation to have creepy similarities to Dickens' *A Christmas Carol*, in which Scrooge was shown scenes from his past, yet Ebenezer could do nothing but stand and watch his past mistakes. Instead, I had been watching Lillian's dark and mysterious past for some reason known only to her.

I glanced back to see if she was still keeping a watch on me, which is what I expected, but, to my surprise, she was nowhere to be seen. People piled in all around me, and I felt I was at one of those outdoor concerts where everyone had been packed in together.

From down the hill I heard the familiar sound of a wagon trotting towards the crowd.

A man's voice shouted, "Prepare the nooses and the ladder and make way for the condemned!" A bell rang three times and the crowd dispersed, making way for a brutish man with hands the size of hams. He had a shaved head, violent eyes and a face resembling a roadmap of scars. By the stoic looks on their faces, all the men and women around me seemed to know this man. The last face many probably ever saw.

Underneath the tree, he was grabbing a ladder off the ground when a young boy stepped out from a group of other lads and, trying to impress his pals, attempted to help him lift the wooden ladder, possibly to receive some gratification from the crowd.

"Step away from me, young'un, or I'll dangle your neck on my ropes next." The brutish man said in a gruff tone of annoyance. Immediately, the young boy retreated over to his four friends, where he was met with ridiculing laughter. The giant man lifted the ladder — he must've been six feet or more — and positioned it against the trunk of the tree. He climbed a few steps and tied a thick rope tightly to the tree branch. As the wagon drew closer, he hastily reached into his pocket and pulled out a black leather garment. The scarred-faced and bald-headed brute of a man had now become the town executioner.

The wagon halted further down the hill and two men unlocked the cage for the two prisoners and forced them to their feet. They both had their hands tied behind their backs and were blindfolded with white, bloodstained rags.

Meanwhile, emerging from the crowd, two men dressed in black tunics halted in front of the prisoners. One of these men walked with a Bible, posturing himself above the masses, while the other held another mysterious book.

"Will the two condemned proceed to follow myself and Brother Godwin up here to the doom hill?" shouted the man, clutching the Bible.

The other priest or preacher turned to face the gathering crowd and presented the ancient-looking book for the people to see. "This, my fellow brothers and sisters," he said. "Is the literature of the Devil himself. His faithful imps walk amongst us in disguise — spreading empty promises. Do not be swayed."

The crowd erupted in agreement, then booed at the two prisoners, hurling stones, rotten fruit and clumps of dirt at them. The smaller prisoner, the child, stumbled and fell a couple of times as she was pushed violently closer toward the executioner's hillside.

"Bloodthirsty town rats," said the tall, slender prisoner. It was a voice I had heard more often than I would have liked as of late: Lillian's. "And you call us heathens? Let my Marina go or suffer an eternity of torment. This won't end here. I'll be back. Back to fucking burn your children's children and theirs after that till the end of time."

Despite her threats, Lillian was thrusted forward by another brutish man dressed in a brown, bloodstained apron, while the blindfolded girl trembled behind them. Dangling past the mask rested her mother's same beautiful raven hair.

"My mama and I have never done anything bad to you people. We have helped you. We brought you useful tonics, seeds and oils from our Romanian homeland. We are not demons. We are good people. We do not do the Devil's bidding. We—"

"Marina, hush, darling," said Lillian calmly. "Do not give these monsters the satisfaction. I know their kind. Be strong, for Mama. We'll see each other soon. I promise."

Marina nodded, sniffling, and composed herself. "Yes, Mama."

Arriving just before the tree, the man in the black tunic, clutching the Bible, shouted. "Remove the mother's blindfold, let this enchantress watch her spawn die at the hands of Christ!"

The hangman nodded and unwrapped Lillian's blindfold. She watched as the man in the leather mask hoisted her daughter on his shoulder, as she thrashed and cried, inching closer toward the tree.

"Mama, please. Do something, please."

"Marina!" shouted Lillian, lunging forward towards her daughter as one of the other burly men held her back. "You'll pay, you bastards. You'll all pay."

Marina sobbed uncontrollably as they fastened the noose around her neck. Lillian shouted, "Keep strong, darling! For Mama."

The hangman tightened the rope, and then dragged the ladder away from her feet. As little Marina swung back and forth, choking to death, the entire crowd erupted with cheerful applause, and Lillian watched as her daughter's body went limp. She released a terrifying scream of agony, one only possibly conjured by a parent losing their child. Falling to her knees, she wept.

The crowd went silent.

After a few moments, Lillian rose from the ground, her eyes filled with a burning hatred. If I didn't know any better, I'd say whoever Lillian had been until then had just died, and someone more terrifying had been born.

Glaring menacingly at the crowd, she screamed. "You lousy, rotten bastards! Putting my daughter to death. Taking the only thing that mattered to me … Just wait. Just you all wait. You think you've won, but you've condemned yourselves to a lifetime of torment. I will give you midden rats real doom. I will burn this place to the ground. I will—" Lillian paused her tirade and homed in on somebody within the madding crowd.

"You. Boy. Yes, you. You, little Judas, standing innocently alongside that old snake of a woman. Did your filthy grandmama enjoy her thirty pieces of silver? Was it worth killing my daughter?"

Some of the onlookers and myself turned to see who Lillian was addressing from the gallows in her final mortal moments. Unable to identify the target of her threats, I made my way over to the left of the crowd, since she seemed to be shouting in that direction.

"Don't ye worry, son," said a slightly hoarse female voice. "The Devil will soon harle her soul back to Hell's fire where it belongs, pay nae notice,"

She was a petite, elderly lady who stood a foot away from me, clutching a young boy's hand tightly in her wrinkled hand. From the back, I noticed the lad himself looked uncomfortable and wanting to back away, with his other hand fidgeting inside a leather pouch tied around his waist.

"Walter Fitz Atkins, you'll pay for the part you played in killing my daughter. Your hands are stained with blood and will be again, boy. I promise you that. I know you're still carrying something of mine. Keep it. I will see it … and you, sooner than you think." Lillian grinned unsettlingly.

The crowd booed loudly, throwing rotten fruits and stones before the executioner doused her in a wooden barrel of tar. Lillian bowed her head and muttered something sinister to herself and, when she looked up, her eyes slowly changed to blackened pits.

The burly men propped her against a wooden post surrounded by tinder. After the man clutching the Bible read her crimes of conspiring with the Devil and the practice of witchcraft, the other brutish man then handed the executioner a flaming wooden torch. As soon as the torch touched the fabric of Lillian's frock, she was aflame, yet did not make a sound.

Amongst the cheering spectators, I stood in silence, averting my eyes after watching her once beautiful face and figure melt away like wax in a flame. As her body charred and hissed, the small lifeless body of Marina dangled from the nearby rope on the tree branch. In an instant, my harrowing view of their bodies shifted and, as if hours had elapsed into mere seconds, night had fallen.

I looked around to see I was still standing on the hillside of Lillian and her daughter's execution. The very same hill where the Victorian Garden Cemetery was yet to be built years later in 1831. Even though it was evening, I could tell it wasn't long after the executions had taken place. Before me, only a few feet away from where I stood, the two churchmen who inducted the executions were chatting with the petite elderly lady and the young boy, Atkins, dressed in a drab, brown tunic.

Whatever betrayal Lillian had accused him of, I now realised, was what led to his own fiery death. What I still didn't know at the time was exactly what that betrayal was. Or even how Lillian herself had managed to return from the grave and ignite the Great Fire.

"Atkins!" I shouted, but to no avail. I know my conversation with him before the Great Fire had been a ploy by Lillian, but I couldn't help but try and help the boy. No one deserved his fate. What I was seeing now was her spirit's powerful replay of bygone events, and I had no choice but to witness it, but it didn't mean I had to like it.

I walked closer towards Atkins, dodging the remnants of stones and rotten fruit which had been thrown earlier. Off to the right, Lillian's roasted corpse was slid onto a long wooden wheel cart by the masked executioner and his burly assistant.

"Excuse me, yes, you two good men of the stake and gibber," asked the oldest-looking of the two clergymen. "May I ask your assistance with cutting this little Merlin enchantress down from her rope?"

"Aye, sir, Reverend Godwin. If you'll give me a minute." The thickset, brown-leather masked man replied with a hint of grumpiness.

"Right, Pastor Baxter, where was I?" said Godwin.

"You were addressing the two main witnesses, Your Grace," said the younger-looking pastor, revelling in the sadistic work of their making.

"Yes, Mrs Fitz and her grandson, Atkins. You both have nothing to fear anymore. The justice of our sacred and holy burgh has been served upon these two wretched planners of wickedness. Rest assured, dears, we know exactly how to deal with the dark servants of the Antichrist."

Atkins' grandmother had enjoyed the day's grim proceedings, by the looks of her cheerful demeanour. "I knew the Lord was taking my hand and leading me to you two men of God," she said in a proud and overly righteous tone. "When my grandson told me about the travelling alchemist devils plying their trade at the Kelvin River common, I knew exactly who to go to. Our Lord guided me to confide in you, Reverend Godwin, and you, Pastor Baxter," she said, bowing her head.

Atkins wiped the tears streaming down his face with his tunic and nestled deeper into his grandmother's side.

"I sincerely hope those are tears of joy, my young fellow," Godwin said, peering down at the wee boy. "It is true that doing what God asks of us is the salvation of all blood, sweat and tears. It is therefore not easy, but we are saved and redeemed by it in the end." Reverend Godwin paused as Pastor Baxter smiled, revealing his yellowed teeth, and patted the boy on the head.

As if he were embarrassing her, Atkins' grandmother scolded him with her eyes, and nudged him to stop.

"My apologies," said the executioner, as his masked assistant hovered by the wooden hand cart holding Lillian's charred body. "May I ask, Reverend Godwin and Pastor Baxter. After we cut down the young lassie, shall we inter her with the mother?"

"With God's good grace, no," Reverend Godwin said with a touch of asperity, and made the sign of the cross. "There shall be no mercy for these servants of Lucifer."

"What are your orders, then, Your Eminence? We still have the burgh hall clerk waiting at the foot of the hill for you to sign off the gallows' minutes."

"After we conclude things, we shall have the little enchantress buried here. The demon mother shall have buried on the other side of the hill. We want to make sure that, even if purgatory befalls them, they suffer for their sins alone and without one another."

"I agree most wholeheartedly with His Eminence," said Pastor Baxter, dressed in the same style of robes as the Reverend Godwin. "If this boy and his grandmother hadn't brought these two servants of Satan to our attention, who knows what evils they might have planned to conjure here, in our blessed Glasgow." Pastor Baxter blessed himself, then licked his lips and patted Atkins on the head again.

"I thank you for these most wise words, Pastor Baxter," said Reverend Godwin. "Now, before we return to our priory, we will proudly demonstrate to the boy a little monastic ritual to calm his mind and show there is nothing more to fear. A simple solemnity which gives warped souls and their malicious tools, such as this harrowing book, a fitting end." Reverend Godwin shifted his gaze towards the headsman. "If you would like to proceed, cut me a piece of this one's noose, please."

The executioner proceeded to cut through Marina's rope, and the poor wee lassie's body thudded onto the boggy hillside. Her eyes and most of her face were still concealed by a white veil.

"Absolute fucking cretins!" I shouted, filled with disgust. I knew they couldn't hear me, of course, but the anger boiled within me, and I couldn't conceal it anymore. "You have the audacity to call yourselves men of God? Monsters, the lot of you."

The hangman then handed Reverend Godwin a piece of twine cut from Marina's rope.

"Please remove her blindfold, I will need that and your blade as well, my dear man."

"Er … yes, certainly, Your Eminence." The executioner bent down and ripped the veil covering Marina's face. Her eyes were closed, and it looked as though she were sleeping. Atkins keeled over, gagging and coughing terribly at Marina's lifeless body. His grandmother paid no attention to this, nor did the clergyman.

A moment later, Reverend Godwin was handed the dagger and face covering. "Come, boy, see this. Hopefully it's not too late yet to draw some blood out of the demon lass here." Reverend Godwin lifted Marina's hand up from the grass and jabbed the tip of the blade into the centre of her small palm and drew blood from it.

The reverend's arms stretched wide as he held the bloodied dagger and Marina's veil in the other. He spoke loudly and full of pride as if addressing a crowd of thousands, though he only had a few witnesses. "We stand here this evening knowing in our hearts that we tried offering you Christ, here in our holy Glasgow. But, in your unsaintly hearts, you denounced him by travelling with the pagan literature and allurement of Satan himself. May you now take his abominable book straight back to him." Reverend Godwin turned to Pastor Baxter. "Open this blasphemous book, any page will do."

Pastor Baxter reached for a dark leather-bound tome lying at his feet and flipped through the book's ancient pages, stopping in the middle of the volume.

Catching a glimpse of the page title, it read:

FVSTIS DAEMONVM
AD MALIGNOS SPIRI

"By splashing the blood of the siren's daughter into its pages, we bind their wickedness and proclaim our freedom from their unholy clutches," said Reverend Godwin, tapping the dagger as flecks of blood stained the pages. He blessed himself and smiled wanly at the trembling Atkins and the beaming Grandma Atkins.

"Thank ye and bless ye again for this great salvation," she said with a toothless grin.

The Reverend Godwin cleaned the remainder of Marina's blood from the dagger with her face veil and a piece of the rope and placed them into the very middle of the old book.

After the ritual had been done, Pastor Baxter snapped the book closed and strolled over to the cart where Lillian's charred body lay. "Now we will see the true salvation of our Lord in the justice we have served here today. Amen." He tossed the book on top of Lillian's carcass and made the sign of the cross.

"That now brings us to a close this evening," said Reverend Godwin. "You may take the boy home now, Lady Atkins. You both have been most reliable witnesses to the actions of these messengers of the Antichrist, and we, the Church and all the bishops of this royal burgh thank ye both again for this."

At that moment, Atkins freed himself from his grandma's grip and raced ahead. It was evident the wee guy hadn't enjoyed the gruesome proceedings at all, and I feared he had had more than enough.

His grandmother shouted after him. "Walter Fitz Atkins! What is with your rude haste?"

"Sorry, Nan, I realised I forgot to feed and water the goats. I'll see ye when you get home," Atkins said, almost down the hill. For a boy no older than ten or eleven, perhaps, I had seen such a look of shame and sadness on his face as he was forced to endure watching such horrific executions ... Just what kind of guilt for Lillian and her daughter was he carrying? I wondered. Was the wee boy forced into making a false confession? What part did he play?

As Godwin and Baxter were now walking off into the vastness of the hillside, chatting merrily about their work, the masked executioner handed his assistant a shovel which leaned against a haystack. "Well, ye heard the reverend," he said. "Get digging and bury the wee lassie here under the tree. The ma I'll take down to the nether meadow over on the west side. The quicker we work, the quicker we get to collecting our coin."

"Aye, I'll have this done for ye fore late darkening time." The way the headman's assistant said 'darkening' came out sounding like 'daurknin'. The dialect was mostly all very broad Scots, it seemed, in these times.

As the sounds of shovelling grinded against the earth, my eyes became heavy, and everything went dark and silent.

Eleven

I assumed Lillian had shown me all she had wanted me to see of her last mortal days. From the lightless void, her pale body appeared a few steps in front of me. She walked closer to me as tears of blood streamed slowly down her face.

"Did you see for yourself, Terry Doyle?" she said, her voice cold and bitter. "The cruelty and injustice me and my dear Marina suffered at the hands of the real monsters of Glasgow?"

"I did, aye." I looked down at the blackened abyss I had been standing on, thinking of Shauna. "Nobody in this world deserves what happened to you and your daughter." I stepped closer to her, directly pleading to any remnant of humanity she may have had left. "How did you get captured? How did this all happen and what does it have to do with me? I'm not responsible for you and your daughter's deaths."

"Back then it didn't have anything to do with you, Mr Terry Doyle, but these days it is all about you and what you need to return to me. I need to bring her back. I will bring her back and you will help me once you've returned it."

"Return what to you? I never took anything from you? Why are you doing this?"

Before I knew it, I was on the tips of my toes, and my arms were forcibly outstretched by her powers. With lightning speed, Lillian closed the distance between us and swiftly wrapped her raw-boned hand around my throat, making me start choking.

"I wasn't always this way, Mr Doyle. I was happy once, very happy. And what no one tells you is that happiness comes at a price. Whatever monster you think I am, I was made into one by the very foul denizens living in your precious city." Lillian grinned, as if an idea had popped into her dark and twisted mind. "I think yet another jaunt down my centuries-old memory lane is in order, Mr Doyle. Then, and only then, will you understand my hatred."

Just as I was on the verge of passing out, she dropped me, and I thudded to the ground.

After a few moments desperately catching my breath, I sat up and reopened my eyes to find myself lying by the side of a gentle-flowing river on a warm summer's day.

I eased onto my feet, brushing the grass stained around my knees, and wondered what past event Lillian wanted me to see this time. Aside from the river, most of the area consisted of rig and furrowed fields dotted with wooden barns, and a mysterious stone ruin drawing me closer to it.

I walked onwards through the tall grass and bramble bushes to where this ruin stood. I am no historian, but from what I could tell this was the remnants of some old castle. Its shape and height were like that of a large tower house consisting of a partially destroyed perimeter wall surrounding it.

The dilapidated condition of the wall allowed me to peer inside the castle's courtyard. The crumbled and jagged stone had been overgrown with ivy, while, across, the grounds were teeming with wildflowers. Attempting to climb over the huge gap in the precinct wall, I tripped over something sturdy and stumbled forward. I quickly glanced down at my feet and spotted a sizable rectangular panel of rotting timber with some lettering on it. Pulling away most of the overgrown grass, I noticed it was an old collapsed signpost, which read:

Bishop's Manse
E Kelvin River Nether Common
Land held by house of Baillie, Glasgow 1533

Within a couple of minutes, I was inside the old grounds. Looking over the water, I noticed a vardo wagon, lavishly decorated with intricate symbols and patterns. Right next to it there was a table holding various flowers and jars filled with exotic bugs and spices.

While it was now brighter and more appealing to the eye, I had seen this wagon only about an hour ago whilst walking to the summit of the necropolis. Even stranger, I now saw Atkins standing next to the horse and staring intensely into a jar of fireflies.

"Apostol has a cut on his leg, Mama," said Marina, exiting the wagon and wearing a decorative purple vest and white frock. "May I read the healing charm from your book and show my new friend?"

"Absolutely not, my darling. We have spoken of this before. When travelling, our book is for emergencies only," Lillian said calmly, matching the same white dress with a maroon vest. She grabbed an assortment of vegetables and herbs from the table and placed them neatly into a wicker basket. "I believe I've told you this many times now."

Lillian appeared more lively and cheerful, nothing like the demon tormenting me with these memories. Her raven-black hair shone in the sunlight, and her sea-green eyes sparkled like light reflecting off water.

Marina hovered by the table and crossed her arms in protest. She was very much like Lillian in looks, and her small downturned mouth certainly gave the impression she wasn't pleased with her mother's decision.

"But poor Apostol has a cut, Mama, and your charm from the book only takes seconds. Shouldn't we help him?"

"Apostol is a strong horse, Marina. He can heal from a little scratch in his own time," said Lillian, curling her brow and looking over to her daughter with a stern, parental face. "Without the ritual." She picked up the basket of fresh vegetables from the table and suspended them on the side of her hip.

"But Mama," Marina whined. "I wanted to show my new friend Walter how we can help heal wounds with your book."

"No more arguing, Marina." Lillian brushed her fingers gently across her daughter's cheek. "You go on now. I'm about to prepare tonight's supper. Walk your friend to the auld gate and you can see him another time, if you behave."

"Fine," Marina added firmly. "Then can he at least borrow the jar of fireflies for a bit?"

"Yes, yes, fine. I can see he's still fascinated with them." Lillian said, then released a warm grin.

Overhearing their conversation, Atkins walked over eagerly with the jar. "I've never seen anything like this. Thank ye so much, Marina's Ma, for letting me borrow it."

"That's fine, child. You enjoy it for a bit. Marina will walk you to the auld gate. Have a good day and I hope your grandmama feels better soon," Lillian said, carrying the basket back inside the wagon.

After Marina and Atkins took a few steps toward the gate, Lillian raced back outside of the wagon, holding a large, ceramic pitcher. "The water, I forgot the water. I swear if my mind wasn't attached to my head ..." She ran her fingers through her hand and glanced over at Marina. "I'll go down by the stream and gather some to boil for our soup this afternoon. You see what happens when you bug your mama on these long afternoons? It makes her not think clearly."

"Mama e proasta today, no?" Marina said then chucked.

"Wit does that mean?" Atkins asked, appearing quite fascinated with the different language.

"It means my dear mama is going a little dim and—"

"Mind yourself, Marina," said Lillian with a tone of authority. "You're one word away from cleaning the wagon for the next month. Now go and see your friend to the castle gate while I gather the water."

"Yes, Mama, right away, Mama. Whatever you say, Mama," Marina stressed with more than a touch of sarcasm, and feigned a courtly bow.

As Lillian made her way to a wooded area presumably near the stream, Marina waited until her mother faded from view and leaned towards Atkins, whispering, "Whilst Mama is gone, I want to show you something. Follow me."

Strangely, I felt a force pulling me in the same direction Atkins and Marina were now running in.

As both entered the wagon, I glimpsed inside Lillian's living quarters, which appeared oddly lavish and exotic. The interior contained ornate, golden symbols covering the dark wood roof and walls which matched those on the outside of the wagon. To the far end, a bed was tucked across the wall, containing plush, red pillows and a silk blanket, with a cabinet underneath. On either wall were thick books and odd trinkets from their travels stuffed on three small shelves. At the centre of the room, there was a barrel-shaped table, draped with a yellow linen cloth and the basket of vegetables Lillian must've placed down alongside a cutting-knife.

I stepped further in behind Atkins and Marina as she eagerly led the boy over to the corner of the caravan opposite the bed and knelt on the floor. "Mama always keeps her book of great wonders in here." She yanked the bottom half of the decorative rug sprawled across the floor and revealed a seemingly sturdy and rather large metallic chest covered with intricate designs and inscriptions, one of which depicted a vast mountain landscape and a skyline where the stars were made of tiny sapphires.

"You may put your eyes back in your head, Walter. This old trunk is worth less than what you're probably imagining." Marina grinned, enjoying the boy's innocent wonder.

"Well, c'mon, don't keep me waiting. Show me, then. I want to see what's inside!" Atkins shouted, unable to contain his excitement.

"Hush, I'm gonna tell you." Marina paused, listening for her mother, then continued. "You remember only four moons ago? I slipped you two old pieces of parchment. It had certain writings on it, but I told you not to worry if you couldn't read it, Mama's pages from her special healing book have a way of reading themselves to us."

"Aye, that's exactly what happened when me and Gran both read your ma's remedy for ankle swelling. My gran, she was shocked at first and—" Atkins stopped and looked away from her. The subject of his grandmother clearly troubled him.

Marina's eyes widened as if afraid she had disappointed him. "What's wrong, Walter? Didn't Mama's magical book work? It works every time for us. We've helped a lot of strangers in our travels. More than I can count."

"It's not that it didn't work, Marina. The voice of the healing magic, or whatever you call it, it read itself directly into both mine and my gran's minds. I mean, we can hardly read as it is. Something else was doing the healing. Some kind of magic." Atkins shook his head, then sighed. "You shouldn't have stolen these pages, Marina."

"Don't worry yourself, Mama doesn't use them as much as she should. People need help and we can offer it. Her book of wonders holds rare magic for good and bad ... although Mama has warned me not to tell anyone that part. But either way, Walter, the book will be mine one day. I have a right to decide who to help, just as much as Mama. Besides, the best part is that you don't have to be Merlin himself to read it."

The boy produced a puzzled look. "Mer ... who?"

"Merlin, the wizard I told you about," Marina nudged him playfully. "I'll teach you the stories Mama taught me, don't worry. For now, at least, tell me your grandmother's ankle has improved."

"I may as well tell you, Marina, since you've become my most cherished friend." His voice dwindled with fear. "My granny isn't happy. She was very frightened by what those pages did, even after they made her feel better. When I tried to tell her it was a simple magical remedy from you and your mother, she knocked the pages out of my hand and clouted me on the ear."

"And the pages?" said Marina, her once cheerful tone fading.

"Don't worry. When she stormed off, I scooped up the three pages and hid them in our barnyard."

"Oh dear, Walter. Your grandmother certainly sounds much grumpier than my mama on a bad day." Marina paused and, as if Atkins' warning was a mere wisp of wind, her face brightened once more, and she said, "You mentioned the crops on your land won't grow, isn't that right?"

"Aye, sometimes it's difficult for me and Gran to feed ourselves on what little grows on our small burgage."

"Let's fix that," Marina said, unlocking the metallic chest. It clicked open, and she reached in with both hands.

"Hold on, Marina. I'm stronger, let me help you with that."

"No need, Prince Walter the Strong and Gallant. I think I have a grip on it." She said, lifting the bulky leather-bound book from the chest and thumping it onto the wagon's floor.

It was Lillian's book alright, the one I saw at the poor girl's execution. Sure enough, it would be around for much longer than both of these two poor innocent souls.

"My mother's beloved Daemoniorum Book," Marina said with a hint of pride. "Its name only sounds scary to ward away outsiders. Only a Craioveneu should possess the book. It has been in my family for many years. At least that's what Mama told me, anyway." Marina heaved her tiny fingers through the hundreds of pages and stopped. "Here we are, pages 597 to 601."

"Marina, stop. Haven't you been listening to what I've said? I told you my gran is scared of whatever magic these pages possess. She thinks it's the workings of the Devil. I don't want to get us into any trouble."

Marina ignored him, and ripped out the pages. Once they were out, she stuffed them into a ragged-looking belt bag Atkins wore around his faded brown and careworn tunic. She then leaned in and kissed the boy on the cheek and whispered.

"This one is called the ritual of Umbra; it recultivates the life of anything on this earth. When your gran is not around, choose your field and simply look at the text on this page. When the words read themselves to you, have a rest."

Atkins did not blink, hanging on her every word.

"The magic," Marina continued. "Consumes your energy. When you return after three weeks, you will have an abundance of fruits and vegetables. After that, your gran should cheer up when she sees you'll never go hungry again." Marina dropped the massive tome back inside the chest and the matter, it seemed, had been settled.

As they headed toward the gatehouse at the south-end of the courtyard, Atkins rubbed his cheek where he had been kissed and smiled at Marina. He slipped his hand into hers and she returned the grin. Arriving at the gate, its latticed bars half intact, Atkins and Marina's cheerfulness quickly diminished. On the other end of the portcullis, two figures, red-cloaked and hooded, emerged.

Marina's eyes flared in alarm. "Walter, who are–"

"Right, gentlemen, seize the girl at once. Try not to hurt the boy, we have someone here for him," said a politely demanding voice that I recognised immediately as Reverend Godwin and his unsettling sidekick, Brother Baxter. The same men responsible for their execution.

Atkins turned toward Marina. "Quickly, run! Get back to your mama." The boy lunged toward the men, attempting to hold them off, and pushed Brother Baxter a few steps back. The holy man, sadistically amused, slapped Atkins and tossed him aside.

"Sir Walter, indeed." Marina said, as she raced back in the direction of Lillian's wagon.

Appearing through the sporadic gaps in the castle walls, five more men, by my count, wearing saffron shirts and brown tartan trews, rushed after her. No doubt some form of hired thugs and henchmen, carrying out the dirty work for the Church.

Near the pass, Marina swiftly ducked as a long, red-haired and scar-faced henchman attempted to grab her. Before the man realised he had missed, she swung a hard kick between his legs and the brute toppled to the ground.

"That's it, darlin, you run on," I shouted after her. The pained look on the henchman's face gave me a pleasant satisfaction and, before I knew it, I was becoming lost in these past events again, forgetting this had all happened and now was nothing more than the bitter memories of a vengeful spirit.

"Get off me" Atkins shouted. "Marina, don't stop. Get your ma."

Behind me, Atkins shoved and pulled hopelessly in the grip of a tall, pockmarked thug near the gate. "Ye best stay where ye are, young'un," he said in a gritty voice. "Or we'll break both yer scrawny legs for ye."

"Mama, Mama!" shouted Marina. "Help, there are bad men chasing us!"

I quickly turned back to see the young lass, only a foot away from their wagon and running towards the woods. Apostol neighed loudly, kicking and thrashing in his carriage reigns.

Soon, another thug with long, dark hair and a scraggly beard quickly closed the distance, wielding a sheathed sword of some kind.

"Mama, help us, please!" Marina cried once more.

As she neared the edge of the woods, the thug launched the sheathed sword into the air – smacking the back of the young lassie's head with a horrible clank, and little Marina Craioveneu fell to the ground.

I stood there, open-mouthed and dreading what I was going to witness next.

"Yes, finally we have her!" yelled Reverend Godwin. "God is truly with us, Brother Baxter."

Baxter smiled in a slimy and crude kind of way, then looked on at little Marina face down in the ground with a horrifying admiration. "With God's good grace and caution," Baxter said, ordering the man who had knocked Marina down. "Hold the demon child right there."

As Godwin and Baxter briskly approached the newly restrained Marina, I felt myself moving quickly along with them.

"This one thought she was faster and cleverer than us, Your Grace." The dark-haired thug said, staring at Marina keeled over and half-conscious. "Even gave our pal Angus over there a good welt right in the bollocks, so she did. If you ask me, she needs a working on this one." He grinned with a savage look and kicked her in the stomach.

The two reverends and the henchmen were circling above Marina like carrion and chatting to themselves when, from the tall grass, a long, pale hand stealthily reached for Angus' sword. Before their gloating faces had time to realise it, Lillian was now holding the man's sword against his throat.

"Step back from my Marina this instance, or I'll sever this nasty pig's gullet right here and now," she demanded.

Immediately, the men around Marina threw up their hands and froze.

"Now, now," Godwin said, in a silvery voice. "May we just ask you to maintain a moment or two of calm, madam." He tilted his head to one side as if to negotiate. "To discuss this situation sensibly?"

"A moment of calm? You fucking pigs do this to my daughter and you want calm? Oh, I'll give your friend calm alright," Lillian's eyes erupted into a maddening fury as she squeezed the blade tighter against the man's throat and a few drops of blood eased from his neck. "The calmness of death, if you don't return my daughter to me and leave this land."

Godwin, his creepy comrade Baxter, and the rest of the men took her threats seriously, it appeared. In unison, they began backing away from Marina, who was now just getting up.

"Please leave my friend and her mama be, they haven't done anything," Atkins said as the men holding him pulled at his arms and shoulders.

Ignoring the boy's pleas, Godwin said, "Madam, before you consider anything more irrational, I must remind you the reason we are here today is because you and this girl are suspected of breaching some very forbidden laws within our monastic burgh of Glasgow. We have evidence of such transgressions and the laws will be carried out to the highest penalty."

I glanced back over at Lillian. Her eyes were a raging storm of desperation and anger the likes of which can only be conjured by a parent protecting their child.

"Nonsense, you foolish priest," Lillian said. "Marina and I have not been here long enough to break any laws. We are travellers. We set up camp, we resupply and then we leave. We have been doing this for many years since we left our home of Târgoviște."

As radiant and even gallous as she looked back in her mortal days, the way she expertly handled the sword and her fearless conviction had the bearing of someone who had killed. And, in those times, I'm sure many had, travelling the wilds.

"What is happening, Mama?" Marina asked as she struggled briefly to find her balance again. Her eyes appeared slightly glazed over. Taking a few wobbly steps, she held the back of her head as a bit of blood dripped down the poor lassie's nostrils.

"My dear girl, are you alright?"

Marina nodded slowly.

"It'll be alright," said Lillian softly. She glanced back at Godwin and the rest of his hunting party with a scornful disdain. "Go inside, Marina, and fetch my book, please. I'll make sure nothing like this ever happens again. Rest assured thy Liber Daemoniorum will make quick work of these ignorant fools. Tenebrae nos celant."

Reverend Godwin, Brother Baxter and their band of brutish men really had hunted a witch that day at the old castle grounds near the river Kelvin, but what they didn't know or even care to know was that Lillian possessed true sorcery, unlike the many poor souls of the time who went straight to the gallows because of mass hysteria and half-hearted rumours.

"Did you just say 'darkness conceals us'?" Godwin asked. "Madam, I will let you know that I also understand Latin." He pointed his finger accusingly at her. "I strongly suggest you put down that sword right now and let this man go, and all of this can be discussed sensibly and without violence."

While hearing Reverend Godwin say these words, I of course knew they were nothing more than the bold-faced lies of a very wicked, old man, as I had witnessed Lillian and Marina's execution.

"Please, Reverend Godwin, sir, my grandma is getting confused these days!" Atkins shouted over from where he stood poised by the thugs holding each of his arms. "What I think she's probably told you about my friends is all wrong. I can vouch for their doing no wrong, sir."

As the naive Walter Atkins tried pleading with them, I noticed Godwin and Baxter exchanging devious looks, which suggested they had detected an opportunity.

"Look, boy, just persuade these friends of yours they must stop their hostilities immediately and come hither to the priory to clear their names," Godwin said impatiently as Marina turned around to look at Atkins.

"Walter? Don't hurt him!" Marina said, losing all focus in fetching Lillian's book from the wagon as she immediately began running over to the boy.

"No, Marina, don't go over there!" I shouted.

"Marina!" Lillian yelled at her. "What are you thinking, girl? Come back over here this instant."

But both mine and her mother's pleas were both in vain.

Godwin craftily seized the opportunity, allowing the wee girl to pass by him just enough that her back was to him, and then lunged for her.

"Marina, look out, he's right behind you!" Atkins yelled. However, by the time the boy's warning was out of his mouth and Marina's smile faded, Godwin's chubby left arm had wrapped itself around her neck and locked her in his grip. Not wasting a moment, he reached his right hand into a leather pouch attached to his belt and withdrew a small, silver dagger and brandished it across Marina's throat.

"Ah, now then, madam. I have your little girly in my possession," Godwin attempted to say calmly, trying to catch his breath in between the drops of sweat stinging his eyes. "Do you not see what can so easily arise when we bring such hostility into certain situations? If you will hear my new demands this time." He cocked his head toward Lillian's sword. "Throw the weapon aside and let our man go. Then walk nicely over here with him and I will let your child and the boy go free. It is mainly you, madam, that we would like to speak with. Come now, let us be civilised," he demanded, caressing Marina's throat with the tip of the dagger blade as she whimpered in his clutches.

"Marina," said Lillian. "It's okay, I will fix this."

"Madam, please. No one needs to be hurt." Godwin told her. He was certainly keeping all his false niceties in check. However, there was something odd about his eye contact when interacting with Lillian. As he spoke, he seemed to be sneaking glances from the corner of his eye in the direction of the wagon where Lillian's horse, Apostol, stood chomping clumps of grass.

"Release my daughter and the boy."

"And what of you? We still require questioning."

Lillian sighed. "I will go with you, once they are safe."

Godwin looked over at the two men holding Atkins and signalled them with a brief nod. At once, the thugs released the boy.

Atkins' eyes lit with renewed hope as made his way next to Marina, holding her hand. He waited as Godwin asked several mundane questions to Lillian. Then, he noticed Baxter's venomous smile widening with every second. Matching his gaze, I myself soon realised why he seemed happy. The boy had opened his mouth to warn Lillian of the impending danger when, from behind, two silent mercenaries approached from the wagon and quickly seized her.

"Tie her mouth shut," Godwin said sharply. "Do not let this treacherous snake utter another word."

"Release the boy," Baxter demanded. "His gran wants the payment … and him."

As I watched Marina screaming for her mama and Atkins protesting, I felt yanked from the world, and it slowly faded from view.

Twelve

The most harrowing aspects of Lillian Craioveneu's mortal days had now been shown to me. That picturesque sunny day when she and her daughter had been captured and demonised by Godwin's Church was now gone. As cold air and the sight of many grave markers and pillars slowly broke through the darkness, I found myself back in the present-day Glasgow Necropolis with Lillian's back to me as she faced the statue of John Knox.

She looked across the hill, appearing to be in deep thought and ignoring the sudden drizzle and early morning mist creeping over the headstones. "Now you may understand why I took my revenge on this rat-infested place so many moons ago," she said with an eerie sense of calm, then slowly walked towards me.

To my surprise, she appeared not like the demon witch I first met, but the beautiful, pale-skinned, raven-haired woman I had seen enjoying her life with her daughter at the castle grounds before Godwin and his mercenaries arrived.

"I understand in a sense. They killed your child, but to murder all those–"

"But nothing," Lillian snapped as her eyes flared back to blackened pits for a moment, then returned to sea-green. "Imagine if it was your little girl. If you had the power, what would you do? What ends would you go to to bring her back? My Marina was innocent. A mere child. Do not tell me you would not seek revenge, Mr Doyle." Lillian stopped and looked down as though ashamed of her temper. "I'm sorry for my outburst."

"I understand," I said, trying to stay on her good side for the time being. At this point she had proven to be a powerful demon. So, the calmer she was, the better my chances were of surviving this ordeal.

"You know, it does not have to be this way. All doom and gloom." Her voice sounded gentle and enticing. "We can work together, darling. It can all go back, you know. I have met the spirit of your Shauna. No little girl should have to wander the other side all alone without her big, brave daddy." Her hand brushed softly against my cheek and she leaned in closer, until her breasts glided across my chest. "Sadly, though, the revival incantation is short-lived. All I need is a certain, special book that you're foolishly keeping from me. Tell me where it is and you'll be reunited with your little girl, as I will be reunited with my Marina."

For a moment, I felt dazed under her honeyed words and I considered seeing my Shauna again. Holding her in my arms. Watching her head off to school. Walking her down the aisle. I missed my little girl and, being a member of this church, I believe one day I will see her again. But not through Lillian's twisted magic.

Mustering my courage, I said, "Your words are weightless. I will see her again soon, but not through your powers. She's better in the arms of angels than in this place with you."

After I said this, her alluring facade quickly changed back to the horrid appearance I had been seeing all night.

"In the arms of the fucking angels?" She roared, enraged. "I offer you the chance to reunite with your daughter. And you go back to believing that two-faced, old bastard upstairs and his illusions of heavenly protection? That same, old, overrated god that refused to save his only son while the Romans nailed him to the cross and let him rot?"

"My girl is better off there than anywhere near you. Now, for the love of God, just what else do ye want from me tonight?"

"What I want, Mr Doyle, is the book you've taken from me. One way or another, I will get it back. Perhaps you'll recall a time when you were only a wee lad of nine and your name wasn't Terrance Doyle?"

"Wit former life, I've always just been Terry Doyle," I told her as her long black cloak flapped fitfully in the wind.

"Gerald Dunlop, Mr Doyle. You know what I'm speaking about. Your biological mother used to call you 'my wee Gerry sweetie berry'."

"My biological mother? You're mistaken, then. I never knew her. I was in foster …"

"Yes, I know you were fostered out to the overly kind and God-fearing Rita and Shane Doyle, who brought you up in Dublin. But something always brought you back to Glasgow, didn't it, young Gerald?"

"Whatever bloody unsaintly entity you claim to be, I honestly think you're chasing after the wrong person's soul. Listen, for the last time, I was never called Gerry or Gerald. I was in care since birth."

"You poor, wee, gullible thing," she said, then mocked me with a frown. "Is that the kind of lies they fed orphaned little ones like you back in the day?"

"It's not lies, take a good hard fuck to yourself." I was so distressed that the anger in my mind escaped to my lips before

I could stop it. The next thing I felt was Lillian's cold and spindly fingers tightening around my throat. Right at the edge of passing out, she released her grip and I tumbled to the ground, choking and coughing.

Her powers lifted me into the air, painfully arching my back and forcing me to face her. "Well, then, you have some fight in you," she said, somewhat amused. "Nonetheless, it seems I'll have to make you remember what your pathetic excuse for a mind has chosen to block out."

Thirteen

Once again, everything around me fell into darkness. When I opened my eyes, I was sitting at a table next to a middle-aged man and a woman with red, frizzy hair. The man was drinking from a builder's mug and quietly reading the newspaper, while the woman was peeking out from a green-covered book and staring right at me.

"Gerald, why don't you tell Dad where you're going for your next school field trip?" Her voice sounded sweet and oddly familiar.

"Aye," said Gerald. Strangely, I felt my mouth move, and then I realised I was seeing and speaking through the eyes of a young boy at a kitchen table with his parents during breakfast. If this was a real memory of my biological parents before I wound up at the orphanage, then I certainly didn't have any recollection of it. I wondered if my childhood mind had simply locked it away and thrown away the key. But for what reason? And what did this have to do with Lillian?

Laying my spoon on the table, I leaned closer toward my supposed father. "Daddy, we're going to Calderpark Zoo on Monday. We'll see tigers, lions, and penguins. And Shaun heard a rumour that a giant snake will be there." I stretched my child-like hands wide. "It's over six feet, Dad, and it's even older than you."

The man slowly peered away from the newspaper and smiled. He was tall, even for sitting down, and lanky. His strawberry blonde hair had been kept neat and swept back amid a set of thick, black-rimmed glasses and a clean-shaven, round face which resembled mine. "Is that right, my boy? An auld snake over six feet, I had nae idea Grandad was now staying at the zoo."

"John, shush, don't make jokes like that in front of him," said the woman, feigning a serious tone and smirking.

John glanced at the clock hung on the wall opposite him, then quickly nibbled an end of toast and rose from his chair. "I better get going, Trish. I got to meet with Bill and somebody from the press up at Cathedral Precinct at half nine."

"The press? What for?" asked Trish, setting her book on the table.

"Something about wanting to know more details about why the University of Glasgow and Headliner Archaeology are collaborating in a dig up at the necropolis." John grabbed his coat and threw it on by the door.

"Dear," said Trish. "Have you forgotten the most important thing before you go?" She pointed to her cheekbone with a playful frown.

John smiled, buttoning his coat. "Of course, my queen, how dare I forget." He kissed his wife gently on the cheek, then tousled my younger self's hair. "You have a good day at school, my boy. Learn everything ye can. If Daddy's treasure hunt goes well today, we'll get you a snake bigger than the one at the zoo." He waved goodbye and shut the door.

My mother turned to me and said, "No, we will not."

That scene then quickly started to fade before my eyes, and within seconds I found myself outside on a bright but windchill day. A dreadful chill raced down my spine after seeing, once again, the Glasgow Cathedral and the necropolis towering behind it.

I wasn't seeing through the eyes of my boyhood self any longer. Instead, I was back in my adult form, witnessing, just a few feet ahead of me, three men huddled around a tombstone, having a conversation. I could hear their voices, but couldn't yet make out what they were talking about, and decided to get closer.

"Like I've told you, we can't allow any press photos, Mr McDougall. At least not until our excavation work is complete," said John, planting his foot firmer on the hallowed grounds. He wore a charcoal tweed-jacket and was conversing with a short, middle-aged, bald-headed man who wore thick rimmed glasses and was dressed in a brown 70s-style suit, sifting through his notepad. Underneath the man's jacket there was a white buttoned shirt with a pointed and tapered collar, like something John Barrymore would have worn at the time, while hanging around his neck was a press ID badge clipped to the right pocket of his suit, which read:

Edward McDougall
The Herald

The reporter was opening his mouth to reply when the man next to John, wearing a beige Crombie coat and light-blue jeans which flared at the bottom over his brown leather boots, finished his cigarette and said, with a gravelly voice, "For now." "Let me and my colleague get up to the site on the hill. We've got a deadline and we need to start the excavation before the end of the 70s, if you don't mind." He held up his hand to stop the reporter from interrupting him. "All you need to know, Eddie, is that the purpose of this excavation is to attempt to uncover any archaeological deposits on the hill in relation to capital punishment. Particularly in relation to the execution of those condemned of witchcraft. After that, and if you're good," he patted the reporter on the shoulder. "We might just give you a sneak peak at the field survey notes."

Eddie huffed a puff of smoke and edged his glasses closer to his eyes. "I don't see why I can't get a few shots of the site for the paper, but I guess the field survey notes would be something. You two drive a hard bargain." He sighed and tucked his notepad back into his pocket. "Very well, looks like it's the best offer I'm going to get."

"It's the best because it is the only offer we're giving you, Eddie," said John, wrapping his arm around his colleague. "Alright, Bill, I think we've told him everything for now. We best start making our way up the hill. Dominic and the rest of the field team are already up there working on the first trench."

Both men turned from the reporter and walked in the direction of the gate, which led towards the Bridge of Sighs and onto the necropolis.

As if a sponge had absorbed the scene around me, everything faded, and what came into view was a frightening vision of a freshly dug hole, about eight feet deep, atop the hill. John stood near the edge alongside Bill, leaning his hand on a shovel, and together they were examining half of a worn casket embedded within the ditch.

"The geospatial data up here is limited," said John, slightly agitated. "We're getting interference. From where, I don't know, but Dominic's grand idea might work. Putting the new Thomson microcam attached with a small flashlight could get the results we are looking for." He rubbed the bottom of his chin, deep in thought. "It's surprising to note the effort to conceal this body after supposedly having burned them alive. Don't you think so?"

"Let me catch my breath," said Bill, setting aside the shovel and wiping the sweat from his forehead. "It's a lot of effort, digging all this for an auld wooden box full of charred bones, Dunlop. Only halfway?" Bill sighed. "We both need our heads examined."

"It's not just any auld box of bones. This one is unlike the others. A great effort was made for this person. Four locks to seal it … doesn't add up."

"You've got a good point. Why lock it in the first place? They did not go to such lengths with any of the others. Maybe this particular grave had a marker at one time to give us a clue about the mysterious soul."

"Possibly, although the missing headstone would not have been for the city to commemorate the person they just accused and put to death. No, if there was a headstone, it would have acted as a warning."

"A warning of what, John?" Bill asked, his voice slightly concerned.

"A warning from the seventeenth-century Church of Scotland, at a time when hysteria about common people entering pacts with the devil was rife. Depending on the seriousness of the accused's sins against the Church, a stern reminder of the condemned person's agonising death served as a warning for others: Do not trifle in the works of the Devil." John pointed to the casket. " It seems we have such an example."

"What severity of sins do you think this one could have committed?"

"Not sure, most of the accusations were ridiculous. Let's just get the darn thing hoisted up and out of that ditch so we can examine it." He nudged Bill and grinned. "Don't get jittery on me. This could be the find of our careers. Put us on the map. What do you say? Ready to make a fortune?"

As Bill reluctantly nodded, both set off toward the coffin and the scene slowly faded.

Before seeing anything, I felt a few droplets of rain trickle down my face as if they were waking me from a long sleep, and I stared directly at the casket, fully excavated. The bottom half of the lid had collapsed as if struck with a steel football, while the top half had been so well preserved that I could decipher some of the engraving:

LILLIAN CRAIOVENEU
EMPTOR DE MALO

Put To Death 1652, Glasgow

My heart sank when I read the name. My father had unearthed the remains of the sorceress manipulating the waking nightmare I had had since encountering her near Glasgow Central. It had become clear; our meeting had been no accident.

"John, I know we're both fascinated by the find," said Bill, hovering by the coffin. "But I think we better move it to the lab, and soon."

John paid no notice, leaning over the coffin and running his fingers through the grooves of the engraving. Aside from breathing, he did not flinch. He seemed fully enamoured by Lillian's casket, deaf to anything but the whisper of secrets it possessed.

"As I was saying," continued Bill, his voice filling with concern. "I really think we should make the necessary preparations to transport the find before we harm its integrity. It'll be better in a controlled environment, eh, John?"

John's eyes widened. "Did you hear that?" He pressed his right ear against the coffin.

"Hear what?"

John ignored him.

"John, is that a yes to getting out of here or what?" Bill patted my father on the back and he slowly roused from his drunken fascination.

John blinked quickly for a few moments and turned to his colleague. "Right, yeah, the transport. I may as well tell you now, Bill. About ten minutes before we brought this baby up, I made some last-minute arrangements with Dominic whilst you had your tea break."

"Last-minute arrangements? And you didn't think to discuss this with me?"

"Cheer up, Bill. The good news is we'll be getting away from these crumbling auld catacombs soon. Dom is bringing the van round to Wishart Street so we can manoeuvre this better down the hill and into the transit easier."

"And the other finds? The bronze cross shaft, the deer antlers and the Norman bone combs, the—"

"Not to worry," John interjected. "They'll be sorted on the other van with Scott and Big Damian's group down at the cathedral. We'll be leaving as soon as we load the coffin."

"Then let's wait for the other van to be loaded and leave together, that way we'll help with cataloguing. Especially if we're going to the lab."

A crazed obsession lingered within John's eyes. "I disagree, Bill," he said, defensively staring at the coffin. "The casket is delicate and we don't want to waste time waiting for the other team. We must take it first."

An awkward silence fell between my dad and Bill.

Given everything that had happened since Lillian invaded my life, I sensed my biological father discovering her coffin had been the beginning of the end for the archaeologist John Dunlop.

Fourteen

The black nothingness around me was once again blooming into colour. I found myself standing on a stretch of pavement just outside a quaint but sophisticated semi-detached house with a garage. I was unaware of what time it was, exactly, but my best guess was late afternoon during the beginning of winter, when the darker nights set in early. From behind, I heard a vehicle's engine getting closer. When I turned around, I saw that it was a white transit van with a gold coin-shaped logo with words below it that read:

HEADLINER ARCHAEOLOGY LTD
Excavating and preserving since 1961

"You know, John, I always thought this job of ours would get to one of us one day," said Bill, stepping out of the van. "And now it's finally happened."

John shut the door and made his way to the back of the van, meeting Bill. "What are you going on about now? All you've done the whole way over here is worry. Relax a little, eh? Where's your sense of adventure?"

"Adventure? Come off it, John. You've just gone and brought a hundreds-year-old casket with a skeleton in it back home from work." He leaned his hand across the back of the van, preventing John from opening it. "And, as if that's not loopy enough, you didn't get one shred of permission to do that, and you're expecting our team and benefactors not to notice it missing from the field report anytime soon?"

"It's just a bit of extra research, purely academic. Away from prying eyes. If anyone comes knocking I'll take the blame. Is that what you wanted to hear?"

"Aye, you're bloody right you'll be taking the blame, ya madman," Bill smiled and shook his head, looking like he should have known John would do something like this. "All I can say from this point on is, I know nothing. Like that wee waiter guy Manuel said on that Fawlty Towers episode the other night. I know nothing."

"Fine, you made your point, you know nothing. Now, are you going to help me get this thing into the garage?"

Bill nodded and released his hand from the back of the van.

"Trish and I, we'll open the contents carefully and we'll have everything photographed over the weekend."

"And back to the lab at eight o'clock Monday morning." Bill said firmly.

"Aye, of course."

The front door of the house opened and Trisha Dunlop walked out towards the van in a black polka-dotted dress. When she appeared at the door to greet my dad and Bill, I saw that she was holding some arts magazine in one hand, and a full to the brim glass of red wine in the other. She looked quite the intellectual type, my mother, but clearly she must have liked to unwind with a bottle of wine now and again. My wife would have got on well with her, I thought.

Admiring her cheerful demeanour, I noticed I had her eyes. A sinking feeling nestled inside my stomach. I had been reunited with my biological parents, and yet, all I could do was stand and watch as their fates were coming closer to being sealed. In most ways, that was the worst of it. Knowing I could never talk to them. Never go back and change what happened.

"Well, if it isn't Bill Clancy nagging away at my husband as though he was married to him," Trisha said, and hugged Bill.

"I honestly feel bad now ye married this one, Trish. He has completely lost his mind these days. Just wait until you see what he has got in the back here."

"Oh, now, let me guess," she said firstly. "John brought his project home with him. An ancient coffin of some kind. Obviously, we are going to remove the skeleton, light our ritual candles and drink red wine from its skull."

"Great, now I know you're just as bloody mad and macabre as him. You two do belong together."

"C'mon, Billy, how about some tea and Irish coffee in the living room? Loosen you up before we move the casket into the garage."

Bill scratched his chin. "Aye, you daft fool. I'm already too involved to back out now anyway," he said as I watched him, my dad and my mother go into the house.

I found myself surrounded by darkness only for a few seconds before I began to see a light again off in the distance. I couldn't see whatever surface I was walking on, but it felt firm enough to continue forward. I honestly couldn't tell if this memory was truly mine, if it had been manipulated by Lillian or if she was just inside my head relighting the scenes for me. Either way, it was unsettling.

I watched as my dad and Bill sat at the centre of my parents' garage under two medium-sized construction lights pointed toward the inside of Lillian's coffin. My dad was transfixed, slowly gliding his right hand against the tattered, black leather-bound cover of Lillian's book, which read:

LIBER DAEMONIORUM

"Easy, John," said Bill, grabbing his friend's wrist. "Why don't we look into this Lillian Craioveneu first, and find out why she was buried with this."

"What more is there to know?" asked John, pulling Bill's hand off him. "We saw her charred skeleton when we opened her casket. We know she was burned as a witch. If you're still so curious, go over and ask Lady Funny Bones over on the table her life story. I doubt she'll be able to tell you much, mate," said my dad, pointing right where I was standing.

His eyes stared directly at me, and I was in shock at first because I thought he could see me. To my disappointment, I quickly realised he had been pointing past me. I turned and followed his gaze, seeing Lillian's blackened skull, ribcage and other bones lying in a heap on a wooden table against the garage wall. What really gave me the creeps was seeing her skull lying on its side right at the edge of the table staring back at me, like a grotesque, ornamental reminder that it's not always a good thing to unearth the secrets of the past.

"Odd," said Bill. "The cover is titled 'The Realm Daemoniorum', but I don't see any names of authors or any contributors to its contents. A family heirloom, perhaps? Passed from one generation to the other?"

"Well, maybe if you stopped interrupting me I could get past the cover and we could find out more," my dad snapped. He stopped and inhaled a deep breath, collecting his thoughts. "Sorry, Bill. But let's not point out the obvious. There's secrets within here. I feel like I can hear them. Something beyond our wildest imaginations. Something mystical."

"Mystical?" Bill furrowed his brow. "John, it's just a book."

Ignoring Bill's numerous warnings and concerns, my dad opened the book to the first page and read:

REGNUM DEMONRIAM ET ALIAS CONIURATIONES

My dad closed his eyes for a moment. "Regnum? The Realm? The Realm of Demons and Other Conjurings … Interesting, I might be able to roughly translate this without referring to Blackwell's Latin Scroll." My dad said, thinking out loud more so than acknowledging Bill.

Hours passed as my dad examined the book with a fervent obsession. His eyes were glued to every page, hoarding over the book with a fierce jealousy. Every time Bill wanted to pull him away or distract him with another topic, my dad scolded him into submission and Bill remained quiet for a time. Then the process was repeated and, with each word my dad deciphered, Bill got more frightened.

"Ah, intriguing. Here is some text in broad Scots. How fascinating. I think the words are 'Thy Liber, Thy Anima', which I believe is Latin for 'soul'. Then after that it says 'Thy Cordis'."

"John, my friend, it's been a long day, do yourself a favour and let's take a break for the night. We'll discuss it when we take it to the lab."

My dad ignored him, and began muttering to himself.

"John, please?" Bill wrapped his arm around him and pulled him gently from the book.

"These artefacts won't be going back to the lab until I have finished my own research. There's too much at stake. She needs me to keep reading."

Bill raised his eyebrow in confusion and, in a panicked tone, said, "She? Who needs you to keep reading? Trish, John? She'd want you to rest, it's late. Not to mention you could get sacked for gross misconduct. Or worse, the police could get involved."

Outside, a strong gust of wind howled and rattled the garage door. John had just turned to Bill with a furious look when the door opened behind him and my mother entered.

"Hello, gentlemen, I would just like to remind my very own Howard Carter and Lord Carnavon that my garage isn't the Valley of the Kings. And in the house there is a wee boy that wants to say goodnight to his daddy before bed after not having seen him the entire day."

The anger on my dad's face lessened at seeing my mom. "You've actually intervened at the right time, darling. I believe Bill here has more than outstayed his welcome this evening, especially with his oh so priceless advice."

Bill threw down his hands in protest. "Look, John, if that's the way you feel, then too bad. I've known you for more than twenty years and something isn't right. You're not right." He rose from his chair. "I'll be on my way. But these remain best sent to the lab. For your own sake, John." He turned toward Trish. "Take care of him, he's not himself."

My mom nodded. "Of course, Bill. But does someone want to tell me what's been going on? I thought this find was supposed to be the highlight of our careers." My mother asked, her once happy mood shifting to a mixture of both confusion and concern.

"Leave it," said my dad. "It's nothing."

Bill huffed, zipping up his coat. "Yeah, nothing." He walked past Trisha and headed for the garage door leading toward the garden side gate.

My mother called after him, to no reply. After Bill left, my mother rested her hand on her hip and turned toward my father. "What on earth have you two fallen out over? You and Bill Clancy have never argued over anything like this before."

"Look, Trish, people like Bill get in the way of progress because they just don't have the balls to seize the moments when they're presented. I think us and him should part ways professionally for a bit."

"John, Bill's been a dear friend to both of us. He's been there whenever we needed him."

"Trish, change the fucking subject or go back inside and kiss our boy goodnight from me. Don't wait up for me. I'll be in later tonight. I need to try and translate this book a bit more." He turned to my mother with a wildness in his eyes. "Can you do that?"

My mother simply stood there, flabbergasted at the change she saw within him. Unrelenting and unapologetic, his face burrowed deeper within the pages of the Realm Daemoniorum as I watched my mother leave him alone with the most dangerous book of rituals probably ever written.

The image of my father infatuated with Lillian's book gave way to another darkened room. I found myself standing over my mother and father's bed as they slept. My dad began tossing and turning so violently it woke up my mother beside him.

She quickly flicked on the bedside lamp and turned to her husband as a pool of sweat washed over his body and he began hyperventilating. Thrashing over the bed and amid my mother's screams to get up, my dad stopped. He leaned forward on the bed, stiff as a board as his eyes quickly shifted from left to right.

"Page 345, Incantation of Renewals," he said without a breath. "Her ghostly shadow will travel the city streets once more. That's it! When the rituals of the realm have been read to completion, she will return in both spirit and temporary flesh."

"John." My mother touched the back of her palm against my father's forehead. "You're burning up. Hold on, I'll fetch ye a glass of water."

As my mother headed for the door, my father's voice steadied. "No, I'm fine." He moved his feet to the floor and tucked into his slippers. "I'll pour myself a glass when I'm downstairs. I need to go back to the garage, there is something in the book I overlooked."

"For goodness' sake, John, it's almost three o'clock in the morning. Can't you leave that horrid thing alone for one day, at least?"

"You don't understand, Trisha." A haunted look came across my dad's face. "She is already half alive. She's coming back."

"Who is, John? Who is coming back?"

"Last night, when I came back into the house, I saw this hooded, pale-faced lady with black hollows for eyes standing in our back garden. I fear she has a hold of me." He made his way to the bedroom door and hugged my mother.

123

At that point I wasn't fully aware of how much time had elapsed since my dad had first begun reading the Realm Daemoniorum book, but I had a feeling this episode of sleeplessness wasn't the first.

"Just when is all this madness going to stop?" my mother asked. "I honestly can't fucking take this anymore. These days you've been a ghost. And when you have been around you're not really there, but mumbling words from that book. None of us can go like this for longer. Gerald is terrified of you these days."

I watched as my poor dad just stood there with tears in his eyes, listening to my mother for the first time in months as a lost and broken man. Without saying a word, he brushed past her, then stopped a few steps into the hallway. "Trish, my darling ... I promise it'll stop today," my dad said, sounding oddly remorseful. "Right bloody now, I'm going down to the garage and ripping that monstrous book to pieces."

My mother's body relaxed for a moment like a weight had been lifted, then she crossed her arms, appearing firm. "Well, I think it's about high time, John."

"Trust me, I know. I was so eager and naïve at first. I wanted this for us," my dad sighed. "I wanted this for me. But you have to believe me, I never would have imagined this book being this dangerous. A dark soul is concealed within its pages." My dad huffed, shaking his head. "I should've listened to Bill all those months ago. He was right to be cautious. He was right about everything."

"What did you dig up that day and who is this woman you keep having visions of?" My mother paused. "Lillian Craioveneu? I saw her name in the garage next to those remains."

My dad nodded. "The book we took from the necropolis is cursed with some satanic ritual. I can't explain it all in detail exactly, but this woman …" His eyes glossed over as if seeing her right in front of him. "She's a dark and twisted soul. She's been whispering to me. Torturing me. Threatening me to read more of it. From what I understand, all it takes is for someone to read its pages for the soul of its last owner to come back. And she is coming back, Trish."

I watched as my mother slowly believed my dad. After watching him for months morphing into this crazed and obsessed man before her, a look of worry nestled across her face. "Jesus, John, are we in danger? How do we put an end to this?"

My dad rubbed the bottom of his chin, mulling over their options. "Forget what I said about ripping the book to shreds."

"Why the bloody hell should we not? Wouldn't that put an end to her, if she has no way of returning? No pages, no coming back, right?"

"No, Trish, we have no idea of what destroying the book will do. It might open a Pandora's box we're not ready to close. I need to buy more time. I need to confuse her. I need to throw her off its whereabouts … it might give me the time I need to stop her."

My dad left the room for a few minutes and returned with a dusty old book. Oddly, it wasn't the Realm Daemoniorum book he handed to her. The front cover of this dusty book read:

Old Fairy Tales
By Ernest Nister

"What are you planning, John?" My mother asked, looking slightly confused until my father gave her a look that made her realise exactly what it was.

"You switched two book covers around and kept the original text instead of just burning it … Why?"

"Two reasons. The first is that this evil spirit's energy becomes powerless after the person or host stops reading the book itself. I even feel better already after ripping the text from its original binding and hiding it away in this for now. The second reason is we need to find a way to understand this better without her knowing. For now, we'll keep it in here until we know how to completely destroy it and Lillian forever."

"But doesn't that mean this thing still has a lifeline to cling to if the full volume of the ritual is still translatable and intact?" She seemed sceptical of my dad's plan for Lillian's Daemoniorum book.

"I know it's not the best. But, for now, no one reads the book. We'll find a way, darling. I promise. Tomorrow I'm going to call Bill at his hotel over in Dublin and beg him to come back and help us. Tell him what a fool I've been."

"And where are we putting the book?"

"For now, let's just keep it concealed next to my old field notes."

"For goodness' sake, John, you honestly want us to put this thing up on the shelf next to our wedding photos?"

"It's just until Friday, until Bill gets back."

"How exactly are we going to stop this evil witch coming in to put a hex on us when we're fast asleep?"

"I don't have all the answers yet, but she can only grow strong again if someone regularly reads from the book, like I was foolishly doing."

"Are you sure, John?" she asked my dad, kissing him on the cheek.

"As sure as I can be for now, my dear. Let's go to sleep, I think I have deprived myself of it for too long."

My real mother and father's voices faded, and so did their bedroom.

s

Fifteen

In the brief darkness shifting between memories, I saw quick, intermittent flashes of blue and a harrowing siren echoing as the image of a residential street came into view. Crowds of people, some older couples and some families with young children, quickly exited their homes, running towards a cloud of black smoke belching into a clear morning sky and gathered around two fire engines and an ambulance outside the home of my biological parents.

Immediately, I sprinted towards the scene and found my parents' house wasn't completely ablaze. It seemed the fire had actually taken place in the garage and the fire brigade, by the looks of it, was finishing the last of the flames. My heart sank and I knew my parents never saw morning – esteemed archaeologist John Dunlop and his loving wife Trisha had died.

It was no wonder my traumatised boyhood mind had blocked out the events of such a day, and the good ones before it. What shocked and angered me the most, though, was when I had to relive the way the police discussed and reported their deaths.

After the fire brigade cleared the scene, right in the middle of my parents' former front garden, two gruff-looking street cops stood listening to a lanky grey-haired man dressed in a navy blue suit, who by the looks of it was CID.

"Well, like I said, I've just been over with the soccos to have a quick glance at the scene and, by God, it's a bad one today, boys," said the CID man.

"Oh, is it, aye?" asked one of the young police constables whilst the other cop beside him remained quiet, appearing hardly interested as he chewed and blew bubble-gum.

"To be honest, boys, at first I was thinking along the lines of an artsy fartsy West End of Glasgow couple. And maybe they had one too many sherbets and started experimenting kinkily and, as we know, accidents do happen. But, in this case, there's no way."

"Aye, you think foul play, then, Chief Inspector?" asked the other officer who was chewing gum.

"No, young man, I certainly do not," replied the DCI firmly. He took a hand-rolled cigarette from his suit pocket and put it into his mouth, and the gun-chewing officer keenly retrieved his own zippo from his pocket and lit the ciggie for his superior.

"Sadly, I think what we have here today is what used to be known in nineteenth-century France as 'Crime Passionel', gentlemen."

The officers exchanged puzzled looks, seeming as if they had the combined intelligence of a dung beetle.

"Come on, gents," continued the DCI, puffing a tiny cloud of smoke. "You must've heard the history of the old crimes of passion. Most of the time the main culprit was a nice bottle of absinthe: man takes a drink, then another, then another, which puts him into a right auld madness, and the man goes home and roasts himself and the missus alive."

"So you reckon they tipped a few and then burned themselves alive in the garage?" The officer shuddered.

"Maybe they planned it to be like a weird Romeo and Juliet suicide or something gaffer?"

"It's a possibility," said the DCI as he exhaled more cigarette smoke. "Or just the usual trouble in paradise. One of them might've been having an affair and one of them decided to end them both. What we do know is that one full petrol can in the garage was used to douse one another." The three of them were now shaking their heads in disgust at the situation. However, what really disgusted me was the last comment I heard this sorry excuse for a cop say about my real parents.

"What a pair of crackpot sickos they must have been. Honestly gaffer, I'm just glad they never barbequed their wee boy along with them."

"Yes, well, the poor wee fellow is actually inside the Dunlop household just now. He is in safe hands with the social worker and our family liaison, Officer Sheila. We will try and get the wee boy the best possible care we can."

At first, I thought I was fainting, but then the bleariness quickly changed to the unsettling image of my eight-year-old self.

I was wearing these little pairs of cords with sandals on my feet and a yellow T-shirt. There were tears in my eyes as I stared at a photo of my mum and dad on the wall. Standing over me, with her hand on my shoulder, was a kind-sounding woman in a brown plaid wool suit. I then noticed my boyhood self pointing up at the photo as though to show the woman something.

"Before they went to Heaven, Mum and Dad said they were going to get me my own pet."

"Oh, that would have been super. You're a lot like my nephew, he loves his animals too. He would have every animal if he could, even those gnarly hyenas. But do you know the best way to collect and learn about strange and wonderful creatures?"

"Travel, like my daddy did," said the innocent boy.

"Well, actually yes, you can travel the world and do all sorts with these wonderful things as well. They're called books, Gerald, and they are not all boring, especially the ones for your age."

What my childhood self said next to the social worker made my blood run so cold that I even shouted for him to stop.

"I would really like to read books like that. Just the other day, when I was looking for my school tie, I saw a fairy tale book in my mum and dad's room."

"Did you, now," said the social worker with widened eyes. She was acting mystified and fascinated for the sake of a child who had just lost both his parents in one day. She was doing her job and doing it very well, as far as I could see. "Well, since you're such a good boy that thirsts for knowledge, how about I take you through there just now and you can show me your book."

"My mum and dad's room is just along the hall. Hopefully when they come back from Heaven, I can read it to them."

"Eh, yes, you could do that. You lead the way, then, Gerald. Off to your book," the social worker said. She took my hand in hers as I led her down the hallway to my parents' bedroom.

Some years after I disappeared, I found out how the book worked its evil magic. I discovered that the book itself originated in the city of Târgoviște around the first century, which today is a part of Romania. Most likely this ancient text was passed down through generations of alchemists, and perhaps not the good kind. Like my father noticed, when someone starts reading the book's sophisticated sorcery like he did, the dark magic from the book's ancient text gradually resurrects its previous owner. When the book fell into my hands as a young boy, I never knew what it was. I'm guessing one day I opened the front cover at the children's home, only to be disappointed. The book never read itself to me. The cruellest twist of fate was that I lost all memory of my biological parents but yet somehow hung onto that abominable book.

When I turned my head to look back at my once stable and happy childhood home, the front door of the house opened, and out came my boyhood self along with the social worker. I held her hand with my left while gripping the cursed book with my right.

The Realm Daemoniorum book would remain with that same wee boy concealed under a children's fairy tale cover for another thirty years. The same book Lillian had mercilessly tormented and killed to be reunited with again. The very book which she would use to revive her long departed daughter, Marina, and enact her eternal revenge on Glasgow. At that moment, I finally understood why Lillian hunted me down outside Central Station. From this point on, her story and mine intertwined.

PART V
THE END IS NIGH

Sixteen

My view of the Dunlop family home quickly shifted to black, then slowly formed into an overcast night sky. I had been lying down on a cold, hard surface with Lillian's pale, distorted face staring back at me. Before I could move, she put the heel of her leather boot onto my chest and began frenziedly stamping.

"Now, Mr Doyle, once known as Gerald Dunlop. Now do you understand what I am fucking looking for? Tell me where you put my fucking book, or I will burn and reunite you with your real parents before morning."

She lifted her foot from my chest as my lungs and stomach throbbed in agony.

"Look, all my life I never knew what that stupid auld book of yours was until now. I hated the thing, anyway."

"Yet you held onto it until it was read by the wrong person, Mr Doyle. None other than your dearly beloved daughter. You let her access the book when it should have been you – the spawn of the foolish and cowardly John Dunlop. The curse was meant for you."

I hated myself just as much as Lillian at that point. The Daemoniorum book with the fairy tales jacket was found in our hall cupboard by my daughter. I can't remember anything of my parents or early life, that life that Lillian so cruelly showed me, but I do remember that day.

It was a Sunday, the day when my wee girl liked to go on these 'house treasure hunts', as she called them. So sometimes me and my wife used to bring her some old boxes of photos, vinyl albums and ornaments to scour through to keep her entertained.

"I found your old book of fairy tales, Dad. Did you like these things when you were younger?" she asked, sitting in the hallway, diving deeper into an old wicker basket and rifling through its contents.

"Wit, do you mean did I like make-believe things? How do you know it's not your mother's fairy book from when she was little?" I asked her, relishing her excitement as she dug through the basket, and walked towards the kitchen.

"It must be yours, Dad. It was lying underneath a big folder thing with a disc in it called the Bay City Rollers. It's with the rest of your stuff."

"The Bay City Rollers?" I shouted to her as I made myself a cup of coffee. "So you're also blaming me for the ownership of that record, aren't ye cheeky?"

My daughter's sweet and innocent laughter died down and was followed by a harrowing scream.

At once, I rushed straight out into our hallway and saw my Shauna sitting on the floor beside the basket of old things, and with the disguised Realm Daemoniorum book lying open beside her. She held up her little hands to show them to me.

"I just tried turning a few pages in your book to see if there were any cool pictures." Her voice became faint and she collapsed backwards, shaking uncontrollably on our hallway floor.

"Jesus, Shauna, what's just happened, darlin?" I ran over to pick her up off the floor. Her hands had turned a horrible purplish colour. Her eyes rolled back in her head as she began foaming at the mouth. I sat her up on the couch, and noticed her face turning the same horrid purple and bluish colour as her hands. It was like my little girl was going through the stages of pallor mortis right in front of me.

As I reached for my phone to dial for an ambulance, Shauna's eyes opened. To my absolute horror, they had turned this inky black colour as a thick green foam dribbled out of her mouth. She spoke to me in a cold, menacing voice I would later understand belonged to the vengeful spirit I would meet in my taxicab a year later.

"Fool, bring me my book and I will spare your child. Bring the book to where most of Glasgow's dead now sleep. For years I have searched for you, Gerald Dunlop, and now you will reunite me with my rightful heirloom once more."

Once these words were out of my possessed daughter's mouth, her colour slowly began returning to normal.

"Did I get sick, Daddy? I think there may have been too much dust in your fairy tale book."

"Don't worry about it, my angel." I said, my hands trembling. "Are you okay now? That's the main thing."

"I'm alright." Shauna inhaled a few short breaths. "When I started choking and coughing, I could see things in my head … bad things. There were all these people running away from this great big fire."

"It's okay, my darling. We'll see the doctor and get ye sorted," I said, then hugged her as tightly as I could without hurting her. "And rest assured, I'll make sure that bloody book is thrown right into the Clyde."

After her episode, it took Shauna less than a year to succumb to a rare disease. At the time, I thought she had had a seizure or begun hallucinating. Never did I think a demon had truly possessed her. And now it was almost like this event had been some wickedly cruel premonition to which I had been too blind.

"But you didn't throw my book into that filthy old river, though, did you?" Lillian asked defiantly as she lorded over me, ready to trample my chest again.

"Nah, you're right, I didn't," I told her breathlessly. "But I should have, you fucking miserable ghostly wreck. I drove straight to the cathedral down there and placed your unsaintly book inside the place, where I doubted it could cause any more damage."

Just as Lillian was cocking her leg back, ready to kick me again, she stopped, then grinned violently. "Right, then, my daft cabby driver, no time to lose," she said. With one magical flick from her hand, she lifted me back onto my feet. She whistled and a booming crackle sounded. "Apostol, here, boy. Mr Doyle needs a lift down the hill to the cathedral. He has something to get."

In a few seconds, Lillian's horse appeared pulling her vardo wagon and stopped in front of me. Before I could say a word, she flicked her hand once more, and a slippery, uncontrollable force hoisted me up by the scruff of the neck and tossed me onto the passenger's side of the wagon.

Levitating gently alongside me, she conjured a whip and cracked it against Apostol, and a thunderous boom sounded. Immediately, the horse broke into a furious gallop, kicking sparks of flame under his hoofs, and navigated along the cemetery pathway. After a few strides from Lillian's hellish horse, I felt a sinking feeling, the same as when you plummet down a roller-coaster. Peering over the side of the wagon, I saw we had lifted forty feet into the air, gliding over the countless headstones mounted atop Glasgow's Dead City.

The ghostly silhouette of Lillian's horse ahead of us pulled her wagon as it buckled and shimmied after several strong gusts barrelled through the city. I glanced down and got one of the worst frights of that entire hellish night when I noticed that the wagon's buckboard I was sitting on was completely gone. I found myself simply sitting in mid-air with absolutely nothing apart from a thirty-foot drop below me and the roof of the cathedral's sixth-century nave.

Lillian erupted in a terrifying laugh. "So, Terry Doyle. I must say, it has been quite the night for precious book thieves like yourself getting their deserved endings."

I desperately clung to the side of the wagon, holding for dear life and praying I didn't fall to my death. "Look, if you're going to kill me, I no longer care, just don't drop me from this bloody height. Wait until we are down on the ground first, can ye?" Unable to take it any longer, I closed my eyes until I felt a rough thump and heard the sounds of hoofs on the ground. Apostol halted outside the main doorway of the Glasgow Cathedral and chuffed a thick cloud of black smoke.

"Let's go, you coward. We have arrived at your final destination." Lillian glared into the night sky. "Just in time for the witching hour."

Lillian leaped off the wagon and extended her hand. "Come, Mr Doyle, it's time for us to be on our way." She said, and grabbed the side of my shoulder, her icy touch almost unbearable to manage. "Don't worry about the fare from the City of the Dead, big chap. It's only fair, since you never charged me in your cabbie," she said, releasing a maddening, ear-screeching cackle.

I ignored her and carried on, biding my time for an opportunity to escape.

As we approached the arched doorway of the cathedral, Lillian huffed. "You know, I sensed you had hidden my book somewhere holy. I can visualise some of the places it has been. It beckons me. But you have done something to it, I know you have. Its voice is weak, clouded by the servants of your God. Those who claim to work in the light."

"Look, I've told you it's in the cathedral. Please, just fuck off and away. Fetch your precious book of mischief or whatever it is. I'm done with you."

"Spoken like a true Glaswegian. But I am afraid I simply cannot bid you farewell just yet."

"Your rotten auld book is inside this very cathedral, underneath the cloth covering St Mungo's tomb. At the lower part of the church."

"I can feel and trust the beautiful power of the Daemoniorum's pages. However, like all gutter rats of Glasgow, you cannot be trusted. You will fetch it for me."

My heart sank. My desperate plan of leaving as soon as she entered would not work the way I had intended.

For you good people here in church today, who have kindly stayed with my story this far, I will now reveal something that I chose not to in the beginning. Lillian had been half right and half muddled when she spoke to me of sensing the Daemoniorum was within the precinct of the cathedral. There was only a fragment of it. Only five pages of the actual book were hidden inside. Out of sheer fear, and perhaps as well due to my religious faith, I hid these five pages inside a decoy book down in St Kentigern's shrine the night after my Shauna fell ill. Not because I knew at the time Lillian Craioveneu was its owner and she would come haunting me. No, it was more to do with a feeling of something ancient and terrifying lurking within those pages. Yet, at the time, I still didn't realise the hold it had on me, leading me to only part with five of its pages and keep the rest with me. In fact, I realised later she must have been sensing the power of its pages calling to her from me the entire night. Lillian knew I hadn't destroyed it. Then again, what she strangely couldn't sense were the whereabouts of the real bulk of the Daemoniorum Book. The rest of her beloved tome of ancient hexes had been right under her nose the night before.

It was now going on five o'clock in the morning, and whatever demonic subliminal power Lillian still had was somehow denying her the ability to see the majority of the pages of her book were zipped up in a duffel bag in the boot compartment of my cab along with Marina's rope and bloodied veil, which she never mentioned.

"I am sorry, but the last time I checked," I said, lifting my eyebrow. "I can't walk through walls or past locked doors. You're clearly the one with the immortal power. Why am I the one that has to break into a locked cathedral?"

"I don't need you to go trespassing anywhere, you fool. Now, be quiet and walk with me this way. I will open the sacristy door of the cathedral with a chap sequence I have known since the days of old."

"A chap sequence, aye? As in something like a secret coded knock? You're serious?" I struggled to understand how this malevolent and powerful spirit couldn't bypass the locked doors herself.

"In a sense, yes. And hold the sarcasm, or I'll throw you back onto my flying buckboard and have Apostol drop you off at two hundred feet in the air."

"Right, sorry. Show me, then, I just want to get this all over with." I snapped my fingers. "If we're going into the cathedral, I'm gonna need my torch from the taxi. Can I get it?"

"A torch for what exactly?" she asked me with a touch of arrogance mixed with impatience.

I knew I had to tread carefully now, especially after the threat she had just made about dropping me from the air.

"A battery-powered torch to light my way inside the cathedral. It's dark and I'm blind as a bat. I'm no good to you if I fall and knock myself out in there."

Lillian glared at me, scanning my every move. "If you plan to foolishly make a run for it, Terry, then I guarantee you have just signed you and your family's death warrants."

"Look, after what you've put me through tonight, Lillian, I know fine well that you are capable of all of that. I get it. All I'm asking ye now is if I can go over to my cab and get a basic handy gadget that helps us modern mortals shine light on the dark to see better."

"Is that so? Yet you just happen to recall having this 'handy gadget' as soon as I want to send you into the old monastery?" Her pallid face and obsidian eyes were still staring me down so much I felt like I was sinking into the ground. "If needs must, Terry Doyle, hurry up and get this mundane light source of yours. Rest assured, I'll be watching your every step."

As calmly as I could, I turned away from her, and began slowly walking in the direction of where my taxi was still parked up at Cathedral Precinct. It was a two-minute walk over to my cab, yet it felt like a lifetime. With every step, I had to endure Lillian's vile threats.

"If you try anything, my dear, your family is dead. I will kill them slowly, painfully, but not before they beg for mercy, not before they beg for death," she chanted repeatedly as she walked directly behind me.

When I reached the boot of my taxi, I felt her cold fingers hauntingly caressing the back of my neck. I opened the back compartment of the cab and eyed the satchel bag containing the majority of Lillian's Daemoniorum book, my torch and the piece of rope and bloodied cloth from poor Marina's execution. I believed these two things in particular could be used somehow to confront Lillian, but not until the timing was right. After all, I was gambling with my and my family's life. One wrong step and Lillian would fulfil her promise. I thought my best chance at that time would be inside the cathedral. It being hallowed ground, maybe it would offer some sort of protection.

Strangely, as we hovered by the boot, Lillian didn't sense the remainder of the book was in the bag. Her eyes darted back and forth like a hound tracking a scent, but in that moment she appeared to believe the entirety of the book was in the cathedral. As if it was a certainty that a feeble-minded, God-fearing man had put all of it in there. Her arrogance and rage, it seemed, blinded her.

"The hourglass on your family's life is almost filled, Terry Doyle. Show me proof of this 'light gadget' or I will slice your throat with my nails right here for wasting my time."

I paused, staring at the satchel. Now was the moment. I quickly scavenged inside the bag without fully opening it and retrieved the cloth, rope and flashlight. As I turned to face Lillian, I tucked the rope and veil into my sleeve and presented to her the torch, shining it on the ground.

She scoffed, and shook her head in disgust. "How primitive. Let's go, you fool." She forced me forward with her sharpened nails slowly digging into my neck, and we walked quickly back toward the cathedral's main doors.

"Somehow, Lillian, I highly doubt it would be in your best interests to kill me," I said, hoping to plead with her in some fashion. "Unless you have plenty of other people at your disposal tonight willing to break into a cathedral, you need me. Plus, from what you have shown and told me, your ever-long quest to reunite with that book hasn't been kind to you, has it?"

"Conversing with me about my book will not make us allies, Terry Doyle. You are my thrall, nothing more."

"I don't intend to be your ally, Lillian. The best I can hope for is to escape with my life tonight." I sighed, wondering if I would. "I just wonder, how did you come back? No one has read your book since my father. How much time do you have to rekindle the rest of the book's powers and revive your Marina?"

As soon as her dearly departed daughter's name came out of my mouth, she pulled me around by the scruff of my jacket collar to face her snarling, pale and distorted face.

"Before I resort to ripping that witless tongue from your fat mouth," she revealed a row of jagged teeth, dripping with a foul, yellow liquid. "Do not speak of my daughter again."

I stumbled backwards against the cathedral's sacristy doors, covering my mouth, and nodded.

"Good, then let me clarify a few misconceptions you obviously have about the Liber Daemoniorum." Lillian walked closer to me, her nails digging deeper into my neck. "After my burning, the embers of my fragmented soul flew into that stupid boy, while other pieces resided within the torn out ritual pages my Marina gave to him. At the end of my natural life, before being burned, a dear friend whom the womanising poet,

Robert Burns, once referred to as 'auld horny' granted me a delicious deal: he would bring me back for a time if I were to burn the holy burgh of Glasgow. He enjoys the carnage and panic, you see, and I got to enact my vengeance upon the city who cruelly put us to death." Her blackened eyes ignited with a spark of flame. "He provided me with a bottle filled with the very fires of Hell, and I used a ritual from the book I had memorised to help the flames spread like the raging firestorm you witnessed."

"But the devil couldn't grant you the power to retrieve your book?"

Lillian sighed and looked away. "That is it precisely. The kind and fiendish man downstairs plays his own game, and we are the pawns. Satan's miracles are short-lived and only for his own amusement. After the fire was done, after I did his bidding, it was back to being suspended in the spirit realm and evading his ire. The only thing which could sustain the immortality I craved was back here on earth and buried within hallowed soil, which I could not penetrate."

"So you were just a long forgotten nothing until my dad came along." I said, wondering what my life would have been like if he hadn't found Lillian's remains.

"Your father tried a foolish thing attempting to hide my book from me. What he didn't realise was that it was already too late. The time he spent trying to decipher it served to slowly start reading me back to life. When he turned his back on my book and concealed it, I was already half-alive and nestled deep inside his mind."

"So your book needs a mortal to reopen it and read its pages?"

"The longer the pages are open, the more I'm restored. However, there is one other small window of opportunity. An ethereal power surges within the mortal world and, after a decade or so, I can absorb this force and temporarily return. That is, if the spectre you see before you were to drastically perish. There are mysteries of the Daemoniorum book that I am still yet to uncover, Terry Doyle."

We stopped outside the cathedral doors. I turned to Lillian, slightly agitated. "So, you possess, curse, and kill people to try and revive your daughter with the pages of some dangerous auld relic that even you don't fully understand. If the book is a lifeforce, could it choose another master or–"

"Enough!" Lillian shouted. "Backstory time is fucking over," she said snappily, and lunged for what I thought was going to be my throat, but instead was the cathedral door. "Old secrets die just as hard as old habits," she said, and effortlessly ripped off a large piece of the Gothic sandstone that formed part of the arched design to the left of the west doors.

She dropped the chunk of thirteenth-century stone at my feet, and I noticed a rusted lever, shaped like a cross, where the stone had been.

Lillian turned and glared at me coldly. "You'll be doing the honours, Mr Doyle. Open it. Now."

Her tone indicated she was not in a negotiating mood, so I reluctantly moved toward the lever. Gripping my hands around its cold and rusted handle, I glanced back at Lillian as she picked up the broken piece of stonework and passed it back and forth between her hands.

"Stop wasting time and open the door!" Lillian shouted. "Or, if you want, I can get to work bashing your bald head with this boulder. Your choice."

This time I dared not say anything in response, and I pulled the corroded cross handle lever downwards toward me. A few clicking noises sounded, followed by a loud boom above the western entrance doors and a slight hiss as if air was escaping.

"Two-hundred and seventy-nine years have passed since I discovered this secret and the old thing still works. Clever little contraption," Lillian said, as though she had invented it herself.

She smiled, revealing the top row of her decaying teeth, then dragged her long, yellow-nailed index finger down my cheekbones, and dug it into my skin. It was all menace with Lillian. "Move it, you Christian shit. Get fucking in there and bring my book back out here to me." Her eyes narrowed and she pointed her finger towards me. "And just remember to keep thinking about your family and friends before considering anything stupid."

Without a word, I nodded, fearful for my family's safety, and continued toward the hallowed place where I had originally brought Lillian's age-old book of sorcery. Something in those mysterious pages had had a hold over me for the first few days after our late Shauna opened the book. I recalled bouts of whispering in my ear goading me to take it out and look at it. Even at work, driving the cab, I thought about reading its secrets. Eventually the dreams came, quick flashes of ancient lands and long bygone events. Before I had even considered what to do with the book, its powers were slowly tempting me into believing I too would become uniquely powerful. Its greatest promises and temptations occurred on the day I tore out five of its pages and removed the Fairy Tales by Ernest Nister cover, revealing its original leather covering, which possessed the texture of dried human skin. Ignoring its hollow promises, I slotted the five Daemoniorum pages, alongside the remainder of a book titled The Pre-Raphaelites, into the fairy tales book jacket and concealed it under St Mungo's shrine.

I pushed open the door and descended three small steps onto the ground floor of the choir. Bracing myself and stepping forward, every possible thought rushed through my head.

What if I were to raise some kind of alarm whilst I'm in here? Alert the police somehow. And what would they do, you daft man. By the time they arrived, Lillian would be gone and on the hunt for me and my family. Maybe leave the city, take Anne and David with me. Start new somewhere else? There's never a shortage of taxis in cities. You certainly won't be driving away in that taxi without looking in your rearview mirror every second for her pale macabre face and black pits for eyes. Then, when you eventually do get home to Anne and David. Just what horrors will await there? The house burned down with them inside? Or maybe David and Anne are still warm in their beds, but with their throats slashed by her long, crooked nails. Every corner and shadow could be her waiting patiently for the right time to strike.

I stopped and turned on the torch, flashing it in every direction. For my family's sake, I decided not to take any chances and walked in the direction of the main choir, doing Lillian's bidding.

Advancing deeper into the cathedral, I passed by a unique seventeenth-century eagle lectern I remembered reading about in the paper a few years ago. The wooden bird seemed to eye me disapprovingly as I walked down the staircase leading to the lower church and the location of St Mungo's tomb.

I felt kind of silly now about bringing the torch, as I could clearly see the red rope barrier, forbidding tourists from touching the ancient tomb. The stone coffin of St Mungo was covered in a light-blue tapestry, and on top of it was an ornamental Celtic Cross and one unlit candle held within a silver decorative candelabra.

I was praying the decoy book was still taped firmly against the original ancient stone casket. As I kneeled on the floor of the lower kirk, I lifted one half of the tapestry cloth up and over one side of the tomb just as my torch flicked once and died. Overwhelmingly flustered, I let the fabric covering fall back into place, got to my feet, and kicked the flashlight across the floor.

I fumbled through the inside pocket of my mud-stained jacket for the zippo I had told Anne was just a memento of the last day I smoked a ciggie. Little did she know that I had felt compelled to retake the twenty-a-day habit after we lost our Shauna. At that moment, I imagined Hugh's wise words:

Sometimes, Terry, you might have to use what's going against you to your advantage. The good Lord cannot fault you for that.

Hearing those words of encouragement from our dear pastor motivated me to keep moving. I quickly grabbed the candelabra from the top of the tomb and lit the wick with the zippo lighter, then held the candelabra carefully as I crouched down with it and placed it on the floor to help light my way around the edges of St Mungo's tomb.

"Please," I whispered to myself. "Tell me the cathedral doesn't employ anyone to do an intricate clean down here." My mind raced with images of Lillian torturing me. "Because, if not, then we better start scouring this place for a few litre cartons of holy water."

As I pulled back the blue drapery once more, the flickering flame of the candle revealed a series of etchings on the ancient floor. Feeling compelled to read them, I recited aloud:

"Saint Michael the Archangel, defend us in battle. Be our protection against the wickedness and snares of the devil;

May God rebuke him, we humbly pray; And do thou, O Prince of the Heavenly Host, by the power of God, thrust into Hell Satan and all evil spirits who wander through the world for the ruin of souls. Amen."

Despite the harrowing circumstances I was facing in the early hours of morning, hints of hope remained. Kneeling on the ground in the depths of the cathedral, I made a final decision then and there. I would embrace and use any higher power of protection this sacred ninth-century site of pilgrimage would offer me against the murderous demon upstairs.

The candlelight revealed what I was looking for. The decoy book of fairy tales, containing the five pages of the Daemoniorum. I sighed as if a heavy weight had been lifted. With a hard tug, I tore off the tape and brought the decoy book closer to the candlelight.

As soon as it was in my hands, I felt a surge of energy come over me. At that moment, even Lillian felt inferior in comparison. Perhaps I could get the book to work for me. To help me stop her. A strange magic from those five pages beckoned me.

"Did you know that, in the first century, your lord Yeshua carried me in his hands as he walked the streets of Jericho healing the sick? I can make you stronger." The eerie voice

whispered clearly inside my mind as if my thoughts and it were one. Fearing its power, I immediately dropped it to the floor and then yanked the tapestry off the shrine table and threw it over the book.

Breathing heavily, I stared at the covered book. This had been a foreboding reminder that the Daemoniorum pages I had wedged inside this copy were just as dangerous as the book in its entirety.

After a few moments, I slowly got back up on my feet, fully wrapped the tapestry over the book, and held it under my left arm. The candle in my right hand lit the way as I hurried back up the stairs to face Lillian. It was unsettling, but all I had prepared were the things I hoped would work against her now.

Going up the staircase, I was hurrying back into the main nave of the chapel when my heart leapt from my chest, hearing the sound of Lillian's venomous voice right behind me.

"I decided to come in for a little visit after all, Mr Doyle." Her voice echoed off the high walls. "And I must say I like your new candelabra. I gather the modern light source you whined for failed you, did it?"

I slowly turned to face her, feeling sickened. " I thought you couldn't enter a sacred place."

She stood arrogantly at the bottom stone steps outside another set of double doors leading to an elevated part of the chapel. Alongside the stairwell, a framed plaque read:

THE QUIRE SCREEN

"Did I say those exact words?" Lillian scratched her nails down the wooden doors as if she was filing them, then turned to me. "I never said anything of the sort, Mr Doyle. It must've been more of your wishful thinking deluding your mind."

"Really? Because I could have sworn you said–"

"And I could've sworn I made a promise to kill your fucking family if you didn't stop stalling." Lillian's head tilted, her eyes fixing on my left arm. "I presume that's my book you have wrapped up."

I inhaled a deep breath, and made a stoic face. "Of course." I said firmly, feeling oddly satisfied at my deceitfulness.

Lillian studied me for a moment, eying me for weaknesses, then grinned. "Right, good, good. You may prove to be a valuable servant, Terry." She released a horrifying cackle. "Come, bring it here, in the altar room."

With my new trusty candelabra in my right hand, and the decoy book under my left arm, I followed behind Lillian as she reached the arched doorway atop of the quire screen stairway and vehemently pushed both doors wide open.

"I'm home!" she shouted, positively joyful. "Move over, big man. It's my turn to reign now."

I kept silent, thinking about Marina's death veil and noose rope tucked inside my jacket sleeve. In my mind, I rehearsed St Michael's prayer with each step and approached the mediaeval pulpit.

Ahead of me, I saw Lillian was now swiftly walking through the reflecting early morning light shining through the stained-glass windows of the quire.

If she's a supernatural entity, why can't the rotten auld witch melt or turn into dust? It's what a lot of the ghouls, vampires and creatures do in the horror flicks when dawn approaches.

"Take out my book from that shabby old drapery," Lillian demanded. "And bring it over here to this lectern. We have matters which need tending."

Before I unwrapped the decoy book, I glanced over at the wooden lectern carved in the shape of a magnificent but boldly-glaring eagle with its wings spread atop a spherical perch. Setting aside the candelabra on the communion table, I cautiously drew closer to where Lillian stood alongside the lectern. My heart hammered against my chest as I took hold of the decoy book and unwrapped the silk tapestry.

"Finally!" Lillian shouted with joy. "After so long, we are reunited again." Her black eyes changed to their former sea-green colour for a moment while her mouth curved like a scimitar in malicious pleasure. "Now, if you will kindly hand me back my book, Mr Doyle, and I shall bid you farewell, for now. Who knows? I may come knocking if I feel the need. I do hope it was as much fun for you as it was for me."

"I hope to never see you again," I said, and flung the book across the altar table.

As the book soared through the air, Lillian immediately outstretched her left hand and, before it had time to hit the floor, grabbed it. "Well, at long last, we will be reunited, my child. On this morning may the spiritum necromantantia reawaken." She placed the book upon the cathedral's wooden lectern. "Noster tempus con, Marina," she chanted repeatedly.

As I slowly backed away, Lillian howled in pain and released the book. "No, no, it cannot be," she said, holding her hands up into the early morning light as the book squirted blood onto her and the lectern.

The time had now come to cling to my last sliver of hope. I reached quickly inside the right sleeve of my jacket and yanked out the piece of noose rope and bloodied fabric from Marina's hanging. With blood seeping down her black gown – I assumed from the five pages inside the decoy book – Lillian's eyes ignited into an inferno of anger and hatred.

"You bastard, you have severed parts of my Daemoniorum book. Where is the rest?"

I smirked, feeling a small semblance of control, and held up the rope and death shroud over the lit candle I had set aside on the altar table. "You're forgetting, Lillian, that parts of you were severed a long time ago."

"How dare you stand there and threaten me with the long-dried blood of my child!" Lillian snarled like a ravage beast ready to pounce. "You put her blood any closer to that flame while these pages are in my hand and it will be the death of you and everyone you love." She said as she tore out the five original pages still dripping with blood. "My dear Liber Daemoniorum, if anything should happen to thee, for decennium may your promise of death hold this enemy of thine until my return."

Ignoring her threats, I began shouting the prayer of St Michael at the top of my lungs as I brought the rope and Marina's death mask directly into the candle flame.

Oddly, neither of them appeared to burn. For a few moments, nothing happened, and then, suddenly, two blue flames erupted from the torn-out pages in opposite directions. The first flame engulfed the Eagle Lectern and then encircled Lillian, sucking her into the wooden sculpture. Despite her curses and threats, I watched as her blackened eyes became the last of her absorbed within the eagle.

Her soul was trapped in limbo yet again.

As I enjoyed my victory, the other flame burst toward me, coiling along the floor like a snake, and wrapped around my legs. Whatever this strange magical flame was, I felt no burning from it as it covered me, but a relaxing sensation, as if falling asleep after a long day. I saw no more and felt no more. No fear. No pain. Only a white light blooming into daylight.

I found myself back outside near my taxi parked in Cathedral Precinct. As confusion settled in, I looked over at the west doors of the cathedral and noticed they were closed.

"Morning, Terry, son. You reckon you could drop me off at Glasgow Central Station?" asked an elderly voice from behind me.

I sighed, welcoming the sound of a voice that was not Lillian's, and turned to see an older gentleman dressed in a radiant white suit with a silver tie. He looked to be around his mid-seventies, with long, dangling grey hair and blue circle-rimmed spectacles which reminded me of the comedian Billy Connolly. His face appeared wise and kind, emanating a relaxing calm.

I paused, feeling as though the harrowing night with Lillian had all been a dream. "Eh, yeah. I was actually planning on going home, pal." I rubbed my forehead, trying to absorb everything. "But I'm going by that way, I'll give ye a ride."

The man gave a warm smile. "That's very kind of ye, Terry, son. Thank you for giving this auld wayward man a lift. I'll pay the going fare rate, by the way, I hope you know that."

"Don't worry about it, it's not a bother." I rustled around my jacket for the keys. Nothing. Then my trouser pockets. Nothing.

I felt the elderly man stare at me, but I was determined not to look up until I'd found them.

"These might help get us going, Terry, son." He said softly, and the sound of keys jingled.

To my surprise, I glanced up and saw the elderly man holding my keys with a pitying smile as if he knew my situation. His pale blue eyes were filled with wisdom as he winked and tossed them over to me.

Catching them, I said, "Thanks, but just out of curiosity. You keep addressing me as 'Terry, son'. Did you see my name on the ID badge hanging from my taxi window or something?"

The white-suited man hesitated for a moment, then grinned. "Come on, Terry, you don't think I've anything to do with that corroded soul you trapped inside the cathedral, do you? Because I am most certainly not the same as her, son."

"I've been deceived a lot tonight," I said, eyeing the man. "How would I know your–"

"Terry, son, what I need to try and explain to you soon isn't going to be easy for you to hear. And I know all about what you went through last night, and what just happened in there," he said with a brief side glance over toward the cathedral.

"That may be, but I didn't catch your name."

"God," he said and chuckled. "You know it's been so long since anyone has actually called me by it." He dipped his hands into his pockets. "I almost forgot it. You may call me Daniel."

"Very well, Daniel, and what are you going to explain to me that isn't going to be easy to hear?" I shouted, frustrated from the night.

"There's no need to raise your voice, son. Save your energy for your next battle with her."

"So you know Lillian, then? You're the one she's sent to finish what she started, yeah?" I clenched my fist, and steadied my feet.

Daniel threw his head back and chuckled heartily. "I have already told you, son. I've got nothing to do with her." He gestured toward the path alongside us. "Look, walk with me a minute and I might be able to help explain a few things about the rest of that wicked book you made sure she didn't get her hands on."

"She did get her hands on five pages," I said, walking alongside him. "Just before I set the rope and fabric aflame."

Daniel stopped and stroked his grey-bearded chin like a wise professor pondering life's major questions. After a few moments, he reached inside his suit pocket and, to my astonishment, presented Marina's rope and veil.

"They don't even look burned."

"They're not."

"But how? I don't understand. Where did you find them? Near where I passed out in the altar room?"

Daniel sighed and placed his hand gently on my back. "I hate to tell you this, Terry, son. But you didn't just pass out in the cathedral quire. You were completely incinerated, son."

Ever since the flames engulfed me, I had felt an ethereal calm and focus which I'd never felt before. I took a step back, shaking my head.

"If it were not for the innocent dried blood of her daughter on these things," Daniel continued, holding up Marina's noose and veil. "The prayer you said, and the limited pages Lillian had, your soul would have been completely erased. You see, what she failed to realise is that the blood of innocence, no matter whose it is, when combined with prayer in a hallowed place, can protect you against any deep-seated evil or dark magic." Daniel winked and pointed upward. "A little protection from the big man, you see."

I held up my hand for him to stop as I tried to absorb it all. "I'm dead?" I whispered. I thought of David and Anne. Of the life I would be leaving behind. The things which I wanted to say, but never had. "I died?"

"It might not make sense to you at the moment, but why don't you hop in the cab? We're going to go somewhere you know and love, which might help."

"Aye, I guess there's nothing for it, then." I paused and glanced at the cathedral doors. "If it's true and I'm dead, then is my body still lying there? I don't want David and Anne to see such a thing if it's identified." I turned, walked with my back toward Daniel, and put my key into the driver's door of the cab.

At once, I felt his hand rest gently on my shoulder as if to comfort me like an old friend. "Look, son. There is no body. No trace you have died." He kindly turned me around, staring into me with his blue eyes. "Just try and take this in as best you can. I know it's a lot, son."

Anger and regret at a life being denied to me because of a vile demon swelled within me. "Some protection, Daniel. I've lost my life and completely disappeared without a trace. Do me a favour now, take your hand off me and kindly go hitch another ride. I think I've picked up enough creeps in this taxi to last me an eternity."

Daniel nodded and released his hand off my shoulder. "Funny you should mention life, son. I said you died, but I didn't say you were done." He winked and released a subtle grin. "You're going back ten years from now when Lillian's powers return. But this time you're going to need a little help from some old friends of yours. Convince them of the horrors you've seen. Let them hear the truth."

"Ten years?"

Daniel remained silent, leaning over and stuffing Marina's rope and veil into my trouser pocket. "You're better off keeping hold of these before we reach the train station after our next stop."

"What stop? And I'm not going to any station."

From his pockets, Daniel retrieved a gold pocket watch and flicked open the lid, causing an immense white light to surround us. Unlike the darkness which pulled me into Lillian's memories, this light was radiantly calming.

Within seconds, I found myself standing upon the altar right here at Millers Park Community Church, with the Crucifixion of our Lord looming above me. The church was empty until a voice said, "Over here, Terry, son."

I quickly turned my head and noticed Daniel sitting in the front row of pews with his arms folded as though waiting for the choir to perform.

"Where are Gloria and Hugh? This is their church, why did you bring me here? They don't deserve to be dragged into this."

Daniel's eyes followed me as I stepped down from the altar and moved closer to him. "Your true friends here at church won't be involved in your battles until ten years from now, Terry."

"Why ten years? What's going to happen then?"

"The pages of Lillian's book have protected her soul, in a sense. And she will return around such a time."

I leaned my hand on the pew's railing. "Protected her? For what purpose?"

"The Daemonorium is tied to her life force and, because of this, she is given time to rejuvenate while keeping her dark magic's connection to the rest of the book. Speaking of which,"

Daniel pointed down at my feet, revealing my leather satchel bag. "I took the liberty of bringing it here for you."

"Are you insane, man? Bringing this thing into my friends' church condemns them to a perilous danger. I don't wish that on them. I won't have them involved."

Daniel rose from the pew and began walking toward the altar. "This is the only way. The book will no longer do any more damage until she returns and calls for it. You are the only one who knows of the danger beset on Glasgow. You are the only one who knows the truth. A demon will walk amongst them once more, and who will be there to stop it? You must warn them, Terry. You cannot stop her alone. Until such a time, you must hide the book behind the cross of the Good Lord, and I will get you out of here."

"And what if I want to drive back home to Anne and David? What if I want to say goodbye to them in person?"

Daniel sighed and came to me, putting his left arm around my shoulder. "You cannot say goodbye, Terry. Your soul is weakened. Your Anne and David will not be able to see or hear you. You cannot say goodbye."

It was at that moment that I finally accepted my death. My mind rushed with a hundred regrets and memories. A cold, sinking feeling nestled deeper inside my chest. I would not be going home. Anne and David would be waiting for the pizza I was supposed to bring, only to find nothing more than an abandoned cab outside the cathedral, as if I had left them for an affair or something. I broke down, releasing all of the pain and hurt corroding my heart.

"You're going to be alright and back with your two good friends Hugh and Gloria very soon, son," he said as I sobbed away on his shoulder. "Right now, you just pick up your satchel bag and wedge it behind the beautiful carving of our Lord on the cross there."

I wiped my face, picked up the zip bag containing the bulk of the Daemoniorum and tucked it away firmly behind the cross.

By the time I pulled my hand away, the walls of my community church had faded into a brilliant white light and, the next thing I knew, I was back inside my cab and parked outside the Grand Central Hotel.

Opening my door, I stepped onto a deserted Hope Street. No noise. No vehicles. No people. It was like a scene from an apocalyptic movie.

"This way, son. Follow me to the station," said Daniel, standing casually by the bronze tribute statue of the Citizen Firefighter.

Much like Hope Street, Glasgow Central Station felt abandoned. The usual hustle and bustle of frantic passengers had disappeared, and our footsteps echoed. Glancing past the old tie shop, we made our way right beneath the station clock, where Daniel stopped and looked up. To my bewilderment, the hands of the clock were rapidly spinning clockwise.

Daniel looked across the emptied platforms. "Nothing to worry, Terry, son. Your train is due in any second now."

"Any second? How can you tell when the clock is going bonkers, man? What's going on?"

Daniel shrugged. "Time works differently for wayward souls passing through, that's all," he said confidently as though this would somehow reassure me everything was normal. It wasn't.

Just as I was about to ask him the time difference for people in purgatorial situations, the sound of a train chuffing forward resounded off the emptied station walls.

"There comes your locomotive now, son. 'The big sleeper', we call her here." Daniel glanced back at me, outstretching his hand. "Come on, take my hand. We are heading for platform zero."

Before I even had time to grip Daniel's hand, he had already wrapped his fingers around my wrist. Together we broke into a sprint to where the cross-country service arrives. Moving past the ticket barrier, I briefly admired the design of the train arriving. Its caboose was a solid vintage gold and its stream-lined carriages had circular, aeroplane-like windows, so that it vaguely resembled the Duchess of Hamilton train.

We stood by the platform as the train hissed to a stop.

"Looks like your carriage of rest awaits you now, Terry, son," Daniel said, rummaging around in his trouser pocket. "This should be enough to see you back safely when the time comes."

"You already gave me back the noose and fabric." I reminded him.

"No, no, I know that. These are some currency notes you'll need when you're eventually back."

Out from his pocket, he withdrew what initially appeared like laminated forgeries of Scottish twenties and fifty notes and handed them to me as the carriage doors of the big sleeper train slid open.

"The money in twenty-nineteen, as you can see, appears and feels slightly different from what it is at the moment," e said with a heart-warming grin which made him look even more like The Big Yin than before.

"Are you a time traveller, then, Mr Daniel?" I asked.

"Terry, son." He chuckled. "I'm afraid there is simply not enough time in the world to explain what I am and how I got this job." He cocked his head toward the train. "You just get on there and take a wee seat and close your eyes. I'll see you again. I love you, son, you've done well."

Fearing I would break down if I were to give the old man a farewell hug, I nodded without a word and boarded the big sleeper.

Inside, the carriages looked no different from that of any other train. There were no other passengers I noticed as I sat on the first double seat. Two seconds later, the doors slid shut and the train bellowed its whistle and chuffed forward.

As the train slowly passed the station, I made a promise to myself to contact Hugh and Gloria from wherever the train allowed me to depart. A heaviness came upon me and I slowly closed my eyes. When I did, my soul rested for ten years, which, to me, only felt like a long sleep after a hard day's work.

When I awoke, I found myself sitting on the cross-country London Euston train making its stop in Edinburgh Waverly. When the train doors opened, I rushed from my seat and exited the train alongside a large group of commuters. On the platform, I checked my coat pocket, and the funds the mysterious but kind Daniel had given me were there. I navigated through the waves of people along Edinburgh's Royal Mile on the 28th September 2019, just last week. After finding a hotel with the currency Daniel had provided, I checked in, freshened up, and called Hugh at his home.

My part of purgatory was over.

Final Intermission & Closing Prayers

Terry addressed Hugh, Gloria and the few remaining churchgoers, including Delilah Duncan, who had loyally stayed seated within the church. "And so, my friends, concludes the story of how I was forced to leave my family and Glasgow for so long. Yes, it's a very bizarre and difficult story to believe, but I needed to warn you all of the impending dangers ahead and clear my name. Finally, I want to thank all of you who have stayed and listened until the end."

A brief silence fell as a mix of confusion and derision lingered among the churchgoers' faces, followed by muttered whispers within the pews. Hugh eased from his chair and walked to the middle of the altar, signalling Terry for a moment, then addressed the remaining members.

"Well, what an exceptional day it has been, with our Terry Doyle sharing his story with us this fine Sunday. We applaud his courage to speak before us today," said Hugh, clapping softly. He was followed by a few other churchgoers, including Gloria. "Unfortunately, my friends, we don't have time for closing songs and prayers today. For those of you who have been waiting, my sincerest apologies. I promise we will resume our usual schedule next Sunday. If you wish, you may recite the Lord's Prayer as you leave, and may God bless you all."

With that, the remaining churchgoers eased from their seats and shuffled out of the pews. The always-knitting Jesse Rhodes, seeming wholly unbothered, finished her scarf while Terry's former neighbours, Teresa and James Dickson, shook their heads incredulously. Glen and Maureen Bell glared at Terry for a moment, attempting to absorb his information, then whispered to the Dicksons, and the hippy bandana-wearing Biddle family raced after their son, who had already been heading for the door. Aside from Delilah Duncan, collecting the hymn books at the back of the church, everyone in the pews had left.

"I'm happy you've told your story, Terry," said Hugh, approaching Terry with Gloria to his right. "Quite a story, I must admit. I've heard of those who've come back after flatlining for a bit, but ..." He rubbed the back of his neck, appearing sceptical. "Well, it's fascinating to hear."

"You still don't believe me, Hugh?" asked Terry, slightly defeated. "And you Gloria?"

"It's a lot to process," she said, tilting her head and looking away. "This isn't something you hear everyday."

"After everything I've said? I couldn't make this up. You two have to believe me."

Hugh patted his friend amicably on the shoulder. "I believe you believe it, Terry."

At that moment, Terry's face hardened. "Very well, then." He stomped past Hugh and Gloria toward the wooden cross of the Lord. After a few moments skimming his hand behind it, he returned with a zipped satchel bag. "For a man of God, ye of little faith, eh?" He offered the bag to Hugh. "Look for yourself, the both of you."

Hugh paused for a moment, eyeing Terry, then unzipped the bag until he saw the very book his friend had described.

The sacrilegious and evil remainder of the Daemonorium book which belonged to Lillian. Hugh and Gloria peeked inside and scanned its contents for a moment, then peered up from the bag, exchanging looks of surprise as if their entire world had been turned upside down.

"We're sorry we doubted you, Terry," said Hugh.

"Neither of us could have imagined it," added Gloria.

Terry smiled with a hint of pride, grabbed the bag, and zipped it up once more. "It's alright, you two. It seems even pastors and firm believers can falter in their faith."

Hugh nodded as he recounted Terry's story in his mind. "My God, the things you've seen. What of the rope and the veil?"

Terry patted the pocket of his trousers. "Safe for now."

Hugh moved closer to him and whispered. "We need to get this away from here and destroy it."

"I agree, especially since Delilah Duncan hasn't left along with the others," said Gloria, huddling next to them. "She's lingering by the back of the church and slowly moving closer. Ever since Terry mentioned how he fooled Lillian in the cathedral, she's been unsettling, to say the least."

"What are you saying? You think she might be *her*?" asked Terry.

"Think about it," said Gloria. "You've told us that Lillian can take on the appearances of other people, and we haven't known Delilah for long. She's new to the church and largely unknown in the community. No one's seen her husband, and she's been hanging on your every word since you arrived."

"My God," said Terry. "I didn't think she'd be here so soon. I thought I would have more time. She probably knows it's somewhere in the church, and has been searching for it."

"Let's just stay calm for now," Hugh whispered as they huddled closer together. "It could be something and it could be nothing." He turned to Gloria, holding her hands in his. "My darling, can you take the book? Keep it safe until Terry and I sort this out? If that Delilah woman so much as bats an eyelid at your leaving, then we can assume she might be Terry's demon lady in disguise."

Gloria nodded. "I don't like the idea of leaving you two. I'll take it and drive as far as I can till you call and tell me it's safe."

"Whatever you do," said Terry, his eyes filled with purpose. "Do not open the book and read from it. Even if it calls to you. Even if it promises your deepest desire. You must resist it."

"Don't worry, love, I have sat and listened to your story today. I know what dangers it can bring." Gloria held her hand to Terry's cheek. "You've been through so much, Terry. But you're not alone, now. You've got us."

Tears welled in Terry's eyes. "You're right, Gloria. Thank you for believing in me." He handed her the bag. "Be careful."

"You two stay safe," said Gloria, eyeing Delilah, then the door. "Right, I better get going."

"One last thing from me before you head out of here." Hugh kissed Gloria longingly on the lips.

"Be careful, my love." She walked hastily towards the church hall's emergency fire doors and exited Millers Park Church.

As soon as the door shut behind Gloria, the seemingly pleasant and elderly Delilah Duncan dropped the hymn books and focused on Hugh and Terry like a panther stalking its prey.

"Where did your wife run off to just there?" she asked, crossing her arms.

"It's nothing," said Hugh. "Something to do with the kids, I think. One of my girls had a bit of a fall over at their gran's house, and might've hurt her collarbone."

"What do you mean you 'think'? You just cancelled the closing hymns and prayers on us simply because you think your daughter might have had an accident?" Delilah snapped.

"Forgive me for sounding a tad harsh here, Delilah, but my personal family matters shouldn't concern you or our church. Now, if you could please make your way to the door, that's us finished up for today."

The old woman looked genuinely disappointed as she headed for the main door without saying another word. Hugh and Terry exchanged matching smiles of relief, realising they had been paranoid over nothing. Then, Delilah Duncan stopped near the door and faced them.

"I must say, Terry, it was rather kind of your preacher to choose to die alongside you here today. Friends like that are a rarity these days," she said as a devilish grin formed on her face.

"Well, it seems your name isn't Delilah, demon," Hugh said, calmly and casually, which Terry found both comical and admirable given their situation. "Right, then, why don't ye just skip the introduction and hurry up and reveal to us how hideous ye became after they sizzled you at the stake all those years back and get this charade over with, Lillian. Who knows?" Hugh scoffed. "Maybe the good Lord will save ye if ya put an end to this."

Might not be the best time to get cocky with her, mate. Terry thought as he stood beside his best friend, fearing what was going to unfold next.

"I think you'll find that I need no introduction, you pathetic holy man. Haven't you been listening to your pal Mr Doyle here, complaining about the tragedy and hell I put him through?" said the voice of Lillian snappishly from the mouth of the elderly Delilah Duncan.

Terry and Hugh stepped back as Delilah grew seven inches taller with each threatening step she took towards the two men. It was now indeed Hugh's turn to finally witness the abominable terror that had haunted and scarred his best friend. Delilah's once dainty, wrinkly hands began transforming into long, pale and spindly ones like that of Nosferatu, and her once kind and caring face shifted and bubbled to make way for the monstrous demon Lillian Craioveneu. Her pitch-black eyes and deathly pale silhouette with bared teeth tore straight through the mask of flesh previously known as Delilah Duncan.

Hugh stood astonished. He couldn't believe that an ungodly nemesis such as this had been hiding in plain sight within his own church. "Dear lord, Terry, she is much uglier than I imagined."

"Aye, I'm guessing that's why she uses all these human disguises."

"Yes, pastor, your broken friend here has experienced my chameleon-like qualities first hand." She snapped her fingers and a long, silky black cloak, which reminded Hugh of a picture in a book he had seen whilst studying the Illuminati at ministerial college, appeared from thin air. "A so-called man of God like yourself surely should always be on the lookout for imposters within your flock." Her eyes surveyed the church, its hallowed halls echoing with her thundering voice. "Where is that wife of yours with my book?"

"That foul book is out of your reach, demon." Hugh told her loftily as he yanked Terry behind him and shielded him from any long-awaited harm Lillian wanted to inflict.

"Very well, boys, you've chosen to die a slow and painful death in church, no less," Lillian said as clumps of old dead skin from Delilah's flesh dripped off her face and onto the church floor, sizzling on the ground. Her pale and grotesque face and dark, hollowed eyes were now completely revealed.

Terry and Hugh backed up another couple of feet away from her.

"Now, now, not so fast, boys. We're going to have a little fun." Her eyes ignited into a frenzied rage, and her nails quickly grew to long, pointy ends. She brandished them as if unsheathing a sword. "Let me bleed you both a little before cooking you alive in this filthy house of God."

Seventeen

L ike everything in this strange thing called life, it happened very suddenly.

Harrowing moans of death escaped from Lillian's hands as the victims of her past bellowed in agony within a miasma of black clouds. Pews were blasted in a bombardment of magical energy and the roof crashed and trembled.

Sheltering underneath a pew, Terry shouted, "She's going for the windows, Hugh! We need to move quickly. Stay low and keep close."

Lillian's long, raw-boned index finger targeted the stained-glass windows behind the crucifix of the Lord hung on the wall. A tendril of magical energy sparked from her fingers and the church's windows shattered into a hail of shards, blowing inwards and collecting in a cloud of glass. In an instant, they rained down on Hugh and Terry.

Lillian cackled in a high-pitched and excited tone. "It's raining glass in Glasgow today. May this treacherous place bleed with the swine which inhabits it." She outstretched her arms and screamed. "Once, I had you in your fields burning and running for your lives! This time your filthy Clyde River will run with your blood as I tear you to pieces."

Shuffling across to Hugh, Terry yanked the pastor behind the altar and they shielded themselves from Lillian's wrath as shards of glass and wood bombarded them.

"Thanks for saving my arse," Hugh said in between short and shallow breaths. He glanced toward the emergency exit, only a few feet away, through which Gloria had left a short while ago. "I think our best move would be to try and make a break for the exit door just over–" Hugh paused, noticing Terry on his knees, clutching his upper abdomen as a stream of blood trickled down his fingers.

A sinking feeling settled at the bottom of Hugh's stomach. He watched as his friend's eyes widened as if staring into another world. "Nah, come on, Terry. We're not gonna lose you now. Not after what you went through to come back to us."

As both men huddled behind the altar, Hugh peeked around and noticed Lillian revelling in the blood seeping down toward the church benches.

"You see how easy it was for me to end your life today, Mr Doyle?" Lillian released a thunderous cackle, causing the church to tremble violently. "You idiotic fool. All you had to do was return a book to its rightful owner, but instead you will die, Terry. Let the blood flow out of you knowing you failed. All of Glasgow will perish. Everything you love will die. Your family and your pastor and his thieving wife will join you shortly."

Hugh tended to Terry, ripping off a piece of his shirt to wrap the wound across his stomach.

"Leave it," said Terry, wincing in pain and offering a look that conveyed he knew there was nothing else to be done. Hugh nodded, watching the blood soaking through Terry's T-shirt, and remained with his dear friend.

After a few moments, Terry's breathing became shallower. "I know you didn't believe me at first, Hugh, but that's alright, mate." He released a guttural cough. "Coming back to our church was the only way of explaining Lillian and the book. I had to come back here because I realised you and the entire city were in danger. I have been so lost ..."

"And now you are found again, my dearest friend," Hugh said, softly. "Go and take your rest, you deserve it. I won't let her get away with this. Even if I lose my life trying. Then I'll be walking with you soon in the light of the Lord. You've done good, Terry. The Lord will see to you."

Terry's eyes glazed over and he smiled. "Shauna, is that you, darling? Come and see Daddy."

Hugh held his hand to Terry's heart, his voice breaking slightly. "She will be so glad to see you. Both of you can now go in peace with the Lord," he said as Terry drew his last breath.

Hugh muttered a soft prayer, then gently closed Terry's eyes and kissed his forehead. Realising Terry's fight had ended and his just begun, Hugh reached into Terry's pocket and retrieved the piece of rope and veil. Stuffing them both into his own trouser pocket, Hugh eased himself to his feet, and leaned on the altar, collecting his strength. It was time to face Lillian if he could. And, if he couldn't, he was willing to stand tall in the eyes of his Maker knowing he had tried.

"Looks like it's just you and me now, preacher," said Lillian.

"He did not need to die," Hugh said, clenching a fist alongside his waist.

"Of course he did." Lillian's voice dropped to a harsh, grinding tone. "He refused me my book. Refused me my vengeance. Do not do the same, pastor."

"I must say, you really are the epitome of the biblical wolf in sheep's clothing, aren't you?" He carefully stepped over Terry's body and emerged from behind the podium.

"I could say the same about you, the-holier-than-thou Pastor Hugh. I know your past, I know what haunts you, what bites and gnaws at you in the night. Do not make the same mistake as Terry. Tell me where your wife is. Give me my book, and you'll live to watch your city destroyed."

Hugh looked all around him. The once immaculate church had been sacrilegiously defaced. Thick strands of smoke billowed from the smashed pews, which had crumbled to a pile of lumber, while glass trickled from the ceiling and tinged against the floor. Hugh glanced back at Lillian. She was a few steps away from him, gripping a blue-coloured tiny bottle with a flickering orangey substance inside. If it weren't for Terry's story you would have thought she held a harmless perfume spray, but Hugh knew better.

"Did this little tincture of mine catch your eye, preacher?"

"It did," Hugh admitted. "I must say you lack creativity, using the same instrument to destroy Glasgow again."

Lillian snarled like a rabid dog.

"Before we get to the final showdown here–"

"Showdown? My goodness, preacher, how pathetic. You honestly think you're worthy of such a fight? You're a frail old man clinging to his holy texts. Sorry, churchman, but today I simply don't have time for unworthy battles with wannabee crusaders."

Hugh shrugged. "No bother. So is that you off, then?" He released a smart-arsed grin that his dearly departed best pal would have been proud of. He wanted nothing more than to fight Lillian for Terry. He found hitting ladies deplorable, as he and his sister Sandra used to watch in fear as his dad battered his mammy when he was a boy. However, this was a demon threatening all of Glasgow, and he would do anything to stop her. He decided to stall Lillian as long as he could until Gloria took the book further away.

"How about you just forget about that nasty, auld, tattered book for a while, and I'll give you one of our Bibles to take away with you?"

"Don't make me laugh at you even more, man of the blood-soaked cloth. Your so-called Holy Bible has caused more senseless wars and misery than the pages of my book ever could."

"Perhaps you do have a point." Hugh tilted his head, watching the bottle carefully. "But anything good can be dangerous when it's in the wrong hands, wouldn't you agree?"

"Never will I agree with the likes of a deluded fucking churchman!" she shouted, and held up the blue tincture bottle in her right hand. "You're all the same. Just like the hypocritical bastards who put me and my daughter to death. All because of my book and their fear of anything beyond their God. I tried to do more good than bad with it. All I wanted was to travel and show my Marina the wonders of the world. But, when we arrived here, she was shown its horrors."

"I gather whatever is in your wee blue bottle is my parting gift from you today, then?"

"Let's just say that sometimes I like to give this fucking world a taste of its own bitter medicine. Show it the same horrors it showed me." She flung the blue bottle past Hugh, shattering it on the wooden cross of the Lord on the wall.

Hugh shielded his eyes from the mounting smoke as the fire began spreading to the altar, and watched as his church slowly burned in front of him. "There is nae salvation for corroded souls such as you, but I will show ye what is just." His anger getting the better of him, he threw a right hook at Lillian's face, causing it to crack like porcelain. She turned without saying a word and shrouded herself within her hood.

"That's for Terry, you demonic shit." Eager to see his handiwork, he pulled back her hood, and froze. Lillian's features had shifted to the sobbing face of his vanished half-sister, Sandra.

"Why did you hit me that night, Hugh?" Lillian said in Sandra's soft, gentle voice. "Outside the barrowlands the night I told you I was pregnant." Tears dripped down her face. "It was because you knew it was your child, Hugh. You knew it. It was awkward for us to fall in love. We only had each other. But how could you do this to me? How could you abandon me like our father did?"

"Sandra? Is that you? For goodness' sake, you were my half-sister. It was wrong then and it's wrong now. I hated myself for years after that night. I understand why you ran off, but whatever happened to you, Sandra, I want you to know that it was all my fault. You're the reason I turned to God and denounced my sin."

Hugh watched his half-sister's face vanish in the smoke. Whether it really had been his half-sister's ghost, or just more demonic mischief on Lillian's part, he couldn't be sure. The one thing he was sure of was that he had made peace with this terrible sin he had committed as a teenager and had worked every day since to do the Lord's will.

As more flames spread, he made his way through the smoke behind the podium where Terry Doyle lay in peace, the heat of the flames warming his back. Wanting his friend to have a proper burial, Hugh grabbed Terry's lifeless arms and began pulling his body towards the exit. Just then, a writhing tornado of flame and smoke tore down the church aisle, revealing a set of elongated, claw-like hands reaching for him.

"What's the matter, Saint Hugh? Don't you want to spend a little more time in Hell with your half-sister? Or should I say half-lover?" Lillian's voice roared through the thick clouds of smoke.

Hugh narrowly avoided her first lunge, stumbling over Terry's body and singeing the palms of his hands.

"Better watch your step, you almost woke our dear Mr Doyle up." Lillian laughed through the smoke.

Ignoring her, Hugh lifted himself back onto his feet, but Lillian's right hand pierced through the smoke once more and clamped tightly around his neck, throttling him until he was on the verge of passing out, and threw him a few feet into the air. Catching him as he came back down, her dagger-like hands latched onto his collar, then let him fall onto the mic stand Terry had used to tell his story.

As he thrashed in pain on the ground, Lillian's hand reached for Hugh once again, but this time he was quick enough to roll over to the left of the stage and off the edge of the altar platform, tumbling into the small wooden trolley storing the hymn books, which toppled with him.

Hugh found himself lying on his back, defenceless and in agony, coughing and wheezing within the burning walls of the church. He turned and noticed he had landed nearby the fire emergency door, behind which fresh, clean air was so cruelly tempting him.

Mustering his remaining strength, he grabbed a hymn book with his left hand and reached into his pocket with his right and held it there. He thought about how brave and selfless Terry must have been that night in the cathedral, and it was this thought that gave him the only idea he could think of. All he could do now was pray it helped, and boy did he have one very special prayer in mind for this rotten auld bitch.

Hugh coughed and felt a thousand tiny embers pierce his skin as fumes of smoke stung his nostrils. Sliding backwards, he dodged a burst of flames along the floor, then leaned against the emergency exit door. From above, another wave of fire swooped down and singed his hair and the left side of his face. There are no words to describe his excruciating pain. He quickly patted the sides of his face, attempting to extinguish the fire engulfing him.

As he did, Lillian casually emerged from the reeky, vaporous haze, walking unharmed through the flames.

Hugh's eyes narrowed and, battling his infernal agony, he uttered, "Archangel, defend us in battle, be our protection against this wickedness ..." He coughed, unable to continue as the smoke filled his lungs. He withdrew the old rope and death veil, wrapped them around a burning hymn book, and raised it closer towards the flames, threatening to burn them.

"Don't be silly, pastor. Don't use my Marina's blood like Mr Doyle." She glanced over towards Terry's body, burning. "It didn't work out for him. Now, why don't we take this outside, shall we?" She roared and flew straight for him, slamming her fist into his chest and kneeling into his abdomen. Her dive attack was so swift, Hugh hardly really felt his back colliding through the steel double fire doors and out onto the concrete pavement.

"I think it's time I take back these old relics, pastor." Lillian violently pried the rope and veil from his hands and reigned two punches down on him.

"Hey, you there, what's going on?" asked an American female voice, approaching Lillian and Hugh. "The fire department and ambulance are on their way." A crowd of eight bystanders had gathered to observe the church blaze at the corner of Easter Craigs Road near the park at Alexandra Parade as sirens of the fire brigade and ambulance sounded close by.

The young lady, Em, stopped directly behind them and tugged gently on the back of Lillian's black hood.

"Stop that. What on earth are you doing to this injured man?"

The last thing Hugh saw before losing consciousness was Lillian's face morphing into that of a young brunette woman. Her new wide-eyed facial expression of concern appeared as authentic as the woman's standing behind her.

"My God, no. I think this poor gentleman is dying," the newly disguised Lillian said. "I was just on my way to a costume party, and I saw him struggling to make it out of the burning door of the chapel just now. I tried pulling him to the pavement for safety, but I think he needs medical attention."

"You tried to pull him to safety?" Em asked her in a tone sounding inquisitive and peppered with suspicion. "Yet we have all just seen you knocking lumps out of him as he lies on the ground."

"No, I swear," Lillian pleaded, holding her hand to her chest. "You got it all wrong. I was only–"

Em rested her left hand on her hip and pointed the other towards Lillian. "Look, you spooky-dress lady. I think it's best if we just wait for the emergency services to arrive. Like myself, most people are likely going to report what they have just seen you do to the police. You haven't mentioned your name. Who are you?"

Lillian held her clean, normal hands to her face as though upset. "Please, you don't understand."

"I have just asked you a question, lady, who are you?"

Immediately, Lillian removed her hands from her face and showed Em the blackened pits she had for eyes as she scanned the young lady up and down like a snake lying in the weeds awaiting to strike. "Fine, I'll tell you who I am, you little goodie-two-shoes bitch. I'm your worst nightmare come to life, my dear, and if I ever see you getting in my way again, I'll rip your heart out and chew on it."

Em's jaw dropped in sheer horror as she slowly backed away, quickly returning to the other bystanders.

Glaring down at Hugh, Lillian mockingly blew him a kiss. "Get well, darling. There's more coming." She walked over him and off in the opposite direction of the sirens.

In her later statement to Police Scotland, Emily Grace told officers about the surreally wicked-looking woman that had assaulted the pastor and threatened her. When asked where the culprit went, she informed them the demonic lady had turned down a small alleyway next to a boarded-up pub at 1 Kennyhill Square and simply … vanished.

NEWS SCRAPBOOK
From the Big Glasgow Gossiper Online Magazine, November 5th, 2020
COMMUNITY CHURCH BLAZE TRAGICALLY CLAIMS ONE SOUL AND LEAVES PASTOR FIGHTING FOR LIFE

A tragic church fire claimed the life of former local man Terry Doyle and left Pastor Hugh McClelland fighting for his life in a coma. The blaze broke out at Millers Park Community Church in Glasgow. Both men have been hailed as pillars of their community by loved ones. The tragic passing of Terry Doyle, who had recently just moved back to Millers Park after ten years, has left a hole in many hearts within the East Glasgow area. Before the fire broke out, McClelland and Doyle had presented a very special Sunday of worship, with locals attending to hear Mr Doyle's story of how he found his faith again after a long decade of depression …

EPILOGUE

Gloria McClelland tossed and turned alone in her bed as images of Hugh injured in his hospital bed plagued her thoughts. Unable to sleep, like every night since Hugh had gone into a coma from his burns and smoke inhalation, she wondered if she could ever sleep again without him next to her.

She flung her arm across her body and knocked over the bottle of pills lying on her bedside table. Since last month's events, when she left her husband at the church alongside Terry and Delilah, she'd been medicating herself through the days, wondering if Hugh would wake up. Leaning forward on the bed, waiting for the codeine and sleeping tablet to kick in, she glanced over at the satchel tucked in the corner.

All of this for a raggedy book, Hugh? I looked at the thing myself; it took me a lot of courage and a few drinks to open it. And when I did, you know what I found? I found nothing at all. There was no evil magical scripture written within its pages, but a thousand blank ones smelling of musty moss.

Giving in, she got up, picked up the book and opened it. She seemed to enter not a dream, but a recurring memory – the memory of Terry Doyle's funeral.

Rain pounded against the hallowed grounds of St Kentigern's Cemetery. Dressed in her black mourning attire, Gloria walked alongside some friends from her husband's newly charred church. When nearing closer to the rest of the gathering crowd at the graveside, a familiar face from the past caught her eye. Terry's wife, Anne Doyle, was standing stoically alongside their son David. He was a young man now, taller and resembling his father more and more since she had last seen him.

Keeping her distance, Gloria walked on and stood silently behind them. As Terry was being lowered into the ground, she watched respectfully as Anne and David threw in a handful of soil and a freshly-cut rose.

Gloria knew this probably wasn't the best time or place to say hello to anyone after years of silence, but some questions needed to be answered, and she had a few for Anne Doyle. The same Anne Doyle who refused to speak with Terry after he returned, despite them reaching out to her, and who up to this point hadn't returned any of Gloria's pressing phone calls in the days leading up to Terry's funeral.

As the crowd dispersed around the grave, Gloria seized her opportunity. "Ten years ago," she said solemnly, hovering next to Anne and David. "Who would've known we would all be reunited because of something like this?"

"Gloria, it's you?" Anne said, somewhat shocked. Her eyes were puffy and her nose red. "I heard your poor Hugh is still fighting for his life in hospital." She shook her head defeatedly. "What can I say? Words fail me with all that's happened. David and I just want you to know that it was nobody's fault. No one could have known how sick Terry had grown over the years." She curled her arm around David's. "We didn't even know the extent of it until a few weeks ago before he returned. Told by a complete stranger, nonetheless, and then a tragic thing like this happens." She glanced across the tombstones lining the cemetery. "Like our girl hadn't been enough already."

As pellets of rain bombarded their umbrellas, Gloria's brow furrowed in disbelief. "Sorry, what? What do you mean about Terry growing sick over the years?"

Anne sighed and looked back at Terry's grave. "He was our rock at one time, Gloria. A great man and an even better dad to David and Shauna. You and Hugh probably noticed that none of us were the same after we lost our wee girl, especially Terry."

"Well, no, he wasn't, Anne, I know that, but–"

"And he no doubt told you all about the demon lady haunting him? And something else, what was it?" Anne closed her eyes for a moment, trying to remember. It seemed the last few days had been harsher on her than Gloria realised. "Oh, yes, right." Anne continued. "He had to get out of Glasgow because he had this magical book belonging to this witch lady."

Gloria felt sick to the pit of her stomach. She couldn't believe it. She refused to. "But Terry did leave Glasgow after Shauna's passing. For over a decade he was gone from Scotland completely. My Hugh went and met him at Central Station on the day he returned. I remember Hugh telling me that Terry had travelled back up on the cross-country train."

"Away from Scotland my arse, Gloria," Anne snapped. "Terry was staying at some rancid bedsit, run by some woman in Alloway. Ella, I think her name was. Lovely-sounding elderly woman. She called me last month and told me all about this hocus pocus nonsense. That he was planning to come back to church and tell you all." Anne looked away. "Look, Gloria, for years I thought the worst. An affair, murder, kidnapping, suicide … the list goes on. But if it wasn't for that nice wee lady getting in touch, me and David would never have known the truth."

Gloria crossed her arms, thinking of Hugh's condition and how it came about. "And you never thought to let myself and Hugh know all of this? On that tragic Sunday, when he stood up in our church hall and told us his story, you wouldn't even answer your phone. No, instead you left a cold, brief voice message saying you couldn't face seeing him again, and now my husband is fighting for his life because of it."

"How bloody dare you speak to me like this, Gloria McClelland?" Anne shouted as a few people turned, heading to their cars. "My husband's coffin isn't even cold yet. He had mental health problems. He was ill. If you and Hugh believed all of his paranoid nonsense, then, I am sorry to say, maybe you two should've got your heads checked."

Gloria's bedside telephone rang, waking her from the recurring memory. Even though she felt groggy from being pulled away, she was relieved she had awakened before she lost her temper and slapped Anne across the face, which led to Gloria being pulled to the ground by her hair and David having to pull them apart.

"Hello, you've reached Gloria McClelland, may I ask who is calling?"

"Hello, pet, sorry to bother you at this hour. I'm Ella Ogilvie from The Comfy Hoose B&B in Alloway." Her voice was high-pitched and uplifting.

"Right, okay, how can I help you then, Ella?"

"Well, I was calling to enquire about when a family member of the late Mr Doyle would be able to come and clear out his room and belongings. It's just that I really can't hold onto them forever, and I would hate for his things to end up at the dump."

"I'm sorry, Miss Ogilvie, but I am actually not a relative of Terry Doyle's. You see, Terry, my husband's best friend, and–"

"Not to worry, pet. I'm aware of that already. I read about the terrible fire at your wee church last month. It was such a shock when I saw poor Terry's name. May God rest his tragic soul. And, of course, may he watch over your poor husband. I pray he pulls through."

"Thank you for your kind words. It's been a difficult time, there's no denying it. Miss Ogilvie, may I ask how you came by my number, if that's ok?"

"Of course you can, pet. Anne Doyle passed on your number to me the other day. She informed me she had stepped away from dealing with her late husband's estate months ago and that you would probably take any of the clutter he left here."

"Did she, now?" Gloria asked, biting her lip as her anger towards Anne Doyle resurfaced.

"Yes. I must say, love, she did seem very quick to get off the phone. Must be grieving in her own way."

"I'm sure she is. In her own way." Gloria glanced at the ceiling, rolling her eyes. "Right, so about Terry's things. Do you mean his clothes and stuff? Because I can recommend some very accommodating charities that will come and collect his belongings from your address, if you like."

"No, love, I don't mean just some old clothes of Mr Doyle's. I mean boxes of family photographs, and a substantial amount of jewellery, by the looks of it."

"Um, okay, then. I guess I better arrange to get that from you. Even if Anne doesn't want to bother with it, David may want it someday, especially the photo album."

"Absolutely, pet, I didn't think you would want his poor things in the bin. That's why I was calling to check."

"I'm glad you did, Miss Ogilvie. Let's make the arrangements and I'll set my satnav for Ayrshire, then."

"You can call me Ella, pet. It's always much nicer to speak on a first name basis, even if it relates to business matters."

"Very well, then, Ella. You may call me Gloria." She held the phone to her ear and eased out of bed. She was reaching for the bedside cabinet drawer to get her notepad and pen when Ella mentioned something that disturbed her the most.

"Oh, and I almost forgot, Gloria. You can take away those mysterious books he was always crafting."

"Sorry, what books?" Gloria paused, thinking of Terry hovering over a desk concocting the story he told at the church. "Are you saying Terry was writing books when he was residing at your guesthouse?"

"No, not really." Ella paused. "I don't think he was writing these big things, but more like making prop books for a haunted house or film set ... They do look smashingly real, though, he seemed to be good at making them. Big, gnarly-looking leather-bound covers and thick spines. You know, they really look authentic; I will show them to you when you stop by."

Gloria's heart took a couple of big leaps into a rhythm that made her feel spooked and sickened. *Please tell me you didn't make all of that up, Terry Doyle. After we went out of our way to support you and after my husband was burned and now in a coma because of it. Did you have something to do with the fire,*

Terry? How far did your illness go? Were you our wolf in sheep's clothing and we loved you too much to notice it?

Gloria rubbed her forehead, wanting to rid herself of such thoughts. "Miss Ogilvie, sorry, I mean Ella. If you can just give me the address of your guest house, I can make my way through to Alloway for one o'clock on Monday. Does that suit?"

"That would be great, thank you so much again for doing this. My address is Number 6 Widowhood Rd, Alloway. I shall have the kettle on and the biscuits on a plate for your arrival. You take care now, and I shall see you on Monday."

Of all the place names ... Just as my husband lies in a coma in the intensive care unit, tomorrow I will be travelling in search of a road called Widowhood. Please come back to us soon, Hugh, I really don't want to go about this life alone.

No. 6 Widowhood Rd

It was a long drive, and the satnav directions were a tad awkward when trying to locate the best route, but eventually Gloria made it to Ella Ogilvie's address in Alloway. After parking and locking her car, she cautiously walked with her shoulder bag along the overgrown garden path towards a dismally grey two-storey council house with no sign above the front door indicating it was a bed and breakfast.

Gloria pressed the doorbell and its plastic casing fell, revealing three exposed wires, which appeared like a severe safety hazard.

What kind of place were you staying at, Terry? You might've been better off in the woods.

When the doorbell didn't ring, Gloria settled for the good old-fashioned way of chapping the letterbox instead.

For a good long minute, she waited and heard no sign of any movement from inside the house. There were no footsteps, voices, the sound of a radio, a TV or anything. Glancing over at the living room window, she noticed the curtains had been drawn. She reached for her coat pocket and tracked down Ella Ogilvie's number on her phone.

Before she pressed call, the curtains drew back and quickly revealed a slightly sallow-skinned face peeking out at her. By the time Gloria's eyes properly focused, the face between the curtains had vanished.

My mind isn't playing tricks on me, I know someone is in there. I only had two whiskey coffees this morning. Me, Gloria

McClelland, alcohol dependent these days? You better wake up soon, Hugh. I can't stand this world without ye.

Gloria made her way closer to the house's living room window. "Hello, Ella? It's Gloria McClelland here to collect Terry's things." She shouted. "We spoke on the phone last week. I tried your doorbell, but it seems it's not working."

Gloria waited, but there was no response. Three minutes went by, and the rain returned heavier, soaking the back of her coat. She removed the leather glove from her right hand and banged on the windowpane three times.

Tired of waiting, Gloria had decided she was done with this venture for the day and had turned to go when she heard a creaking noise from behind her. The door of 6 Widowhood Road opened.

"I gather you're Gloria, Pastor Hugh's whore of a wife. Welcome and come on in, pet. My fireplace is nice and warm like the hell I cooked your man and his pal Terry in," said a sinister voice behind Gloria.

Immediately, she turned around. Standing at the doorstep to greet her was a thickset woman with short snowy hair, wearing a cherry polka-dotted blouse and baggy black trousers that reminded Gloria of the clothes her own mum wore nowadays. Unlike her mum, however, the elderly lady's face was shrouded by a black-and-red-patterned covering that matched her blouse.

"Hello. Ella, I presume," said Gloria, slightly taken aback by what the older woman had said. "It's nice to finally see you in person. Sorry, but I didn't quite catch what you just said a moment ago. My mind has been fried recently and the car's stupid satnav didn't help the issue."

"That's alright, pet. My cup of tea will sort you out. And I said that I gathered you were Gloria, Pastor Hugh's wife, here to collect the belongings Terry Doyle left behind."

Gloria sighed in relief. "Of course, yes, I am."

Ella gestured her hand forward past the door. "Then come on in and warm up by the fireplace for a wee bit, then we'll go through the boxes."

"Thank you very much, I was really starting to get soaked out here," said Gloria, following Ella into the dim and damp-smelling hallway of her home. "You know, I tried the doorbell and then tried chapping the window after I thought you had seen me from there."

"Sorry, love, I think you're mistaken. I certainly didn't look out of any window. I was in the back of the house when I heard your knocking. I've been making a big pot of Raduati soup for my lassie Maria, who is coming over later tonight."

"Really? Because I could have sworn I saw somebody–"

"Anyway," Ella smiled as if to halt the questions. "Living room is just through here to our right. I dare say you'll be glad of my fire, warms the bones right up and then some."

The living room was lit with candles sticking out from the mouth of wine bottles lining the mantelpiece and by a roaring fire. In the middle of the room was a star-shaped, wooden table with an ornamental silver horse figurine at its centre. Gloria quickly noticed its left hoof raised threateningly over a red-covered copy of the New Testament laying on the table as if ready to stomp it. Next to the table was an antique-looking chair, a black bin, and a large cardboard box that had recently been opened.

As Ella entered further into the room, she gestured for Gloria to take a seat on a small, sheet-covered settee over by the curtain-drawn window. "There you are, pet. Just sit back and get nice and comfy."

Strangely, Gloria sensed that beneath Ella Ogilvie's face covering there might have been a sly grin lurking.

"Good to get a wee sit, isn't it?" Ella asked, sitting on the armchair across from her. "Our tea is just brewing, I'll fetch it from the kitchen in a wee minute."

Gloria tried to sit upright on the slippery material covering the settee. "Thank you, Ella. It's nice to sit down and warm up, especially away from the weather outside."

"It's miserable, isn't it? But, then again, I imagine every day is a misery for you … since your husband is in hospital half-sizzled. There'll be no more erotic nights for a good while now, young lady," Ella said casually.

Gloria tucked her hand underneath her lap and clenched her fist. She wanted Terry's things and, more importantly, she wanted answers. All she could do was ignore the absolutely disgusting, disrespectful comment made by this bonkers lady and leave as quickly as possible.

"Yes, my Hugh was the pastor of Millers Park Church in Glasgow. We married young, but everything seemed to work fine for us over the years. We're best pals as well as man and wife."

"Isn't that just dead nice? In a soppy sort of way, that is. Nae offence when I said the word 'dead', pet." Ella knocked on the armrest. "Touch wood he doesn't snuff it anytime soon."

"No, that's fine, don't worry about it," Gloria told her, clenching her fist tighter under her lap.

"Apologies, pet, it's just my lingo at times. I should've known bringing up the word 'dead' would no doubt upset any woman whose man is in a coma, fighting for his life." Ella clapped and eased from her seat. "Right, I better go and get us that pot of tea, eh."

Gloria sat terribly uncomfortable with the shoulder bag carrying Terry Doyle's supposedly cursed book. As Ella left, she reconsidered bringing the subject up with the nut case of a woman who had told her on the phone Terry had made these replica books all the time.

"Here we are now," she heard Ella say from the hallway as she carried two purple teacups into the living room and placed one cup on the table in front of Gloria, then sat down with her cup.

"Now, that's just hellishly divine," Ella said after raising the teacup to her face covering and sniffing her tea. She released a high-pitch cackle. "But I went and stupidly forgot again, didn't I?"

"What did you forget, then?" Gloria asked in an attempt to act normal around this woman.

"I went and forgot I can't drink hot liquids anymore. Face leprosy, pet. If I took so much as a sip of tea, the rest of my dirty, old lips might fall right into my cup ..." she said, cackling with such insane laughter the candles flickered and the flames within the fireplace hissed.

Gloria pretended to sip from her own cup. "What a lovely cup of tea you make, Ella. Well, then, if you like I can take Terry's box and other things. And I shall get out of your hair so you can have supper with your daughter later."

Ella sat in silence for a few moments, staring at Gloria. It was like she could sense her anxiousness and wanted to savour it for a bit longer. She leaned over and reached down for the cardboard box at the side of her armchair. After a brief rummage through it, she pulled out a large brown leather-bound book.

"I may as well ask you about this, pet, but do you have a book that's very similar to this one in your satchel?"

"That's correct, I brought Terry's demon book with me. I wanted to compare the ones you have here with this one. His story seemed convincing, and I just needed to see the hoax myself, Miss Ogilvie."

"That's alright, pet, and remember you can call me Ella. Just goes to show ye, you think you know someone, then it turns out they're nothing but an imposter." Ella paused for a moment. "Do you think Terry had something to do with your church blaze?"

Yes, I have thought about it, but I am not going to sit here all day and discuss my worries with you, Ella.

"I really don't know," said Gloria. "I don't know what happened, but he made it all sound so real." She sighed, thinking of Hugh. "I just need answers."

"I knew Terry was a bit of a lost soul. That's why I let him settle in the room upstairs. He seemed broken. I even made him his own set of keys to come and go as he liked. I remember the day I knocked on his door upstairs to ask if he wanted a bowl of my soup, a family recipe, from Romania. My goodness," Ella waved her hand in front of her face as if shooing away a foul odour. "The smell of the glue and paint nearly knocked me over. That's when he first showed me the books he had been making. Very driven and focused, Terry had been. Although a bit mad."

"I see, so I am gathering that he was nice to you when he lodged here, then?"

"Oh yes, pet, I never had any bother with Terry. He mostly kept to himself." Ella's face covering shifted towards Gloria's satchel. "Would it be alright if I saw the prop book you brought along with you?"

Gloria exhaled a long, deep breath, as if the truth had finally sunk in. "I don't see why not. You've no doubt found a few of them when clearing out his room." She removed the book from the satchel bag and offered it to the elderly woman. "Is it the same as the others?"

Ignoring Gloria, Ella snatched the book, placed it on her lap, and opened it. All of the light in the room was suddenly extinguished and an eerie silence fell. Ella Ogilvie and the book had vanished.

After a few unsettling moments, the fireplace ignited with a raging fire. "At long last," said a voice echoing from the blaze. "Aperi vulnera tua. Open thy wounds and fill with our enemy's blood. Ut vivimus iterum. May we live on to haunt their cruel shadowy hearts eternally."

Gloria's heart sank as she realised Terry's story had been anything but a fantasy. She was backpedalling closer to the door when the scowling face of a woman formed within the flames.

"You are one stupid, stupid whore, Gloria McClelland. Did you honestly think I was just a figment of Terry Doyle's imagination? That he was to blame for your pathetic church's burning? How simple you mortals all are! You thought just because you couldn't see any writing in my book that it simply wasn't real? The Realm Daemoniorum doesn't read for just anyone. I am its master. It obeys me. When will you all learn? I am the judge, the jury and the executioner."

Gloria stood frozen in horror, knowing this could be the end of her.

"Thank you for returning my book. Although I do wish it had been more of a challenge. You so easily returned it to the feeble, elderly Ella." The voice released a high-pitch cackle, causing the flames to dance upward over the fireplace. "Gormless Gloria, the stupid whore of a dying preacher. I'm going to let you rot and live on with a husband who will forever be a vegetable and a constant reminder that you have failed. Watch and witness my power. Watch as I bring you all to your knees." Lillian revealed her sinister face within the fire, and in an instant the flames turned to a dark shade of red before they snuffed themselves out.

Fearing for her life, Gloria bolted out of the living room and into the hallway. To her astonishment, she saw the front door of the house was no longer there, only the wild breeze barreling through the doorless frame. Rushing past the door and into the overgrown garden, she pricked her legs against the spiked grass settling at her waist and headed for her car.

As she turned her keys into the ignition, she glanced back at the house, noticing there were no windows with the curtains drawn, but instead metal panels barring all the windows, and realised the house had most likely been uninhabited for years. Shaking her head in disbelief, she started the engine and peeled onto the street as fast as she could.

She had finally met the unstoppable demon that had critically injured her husband and ended the life of their good friend Terry Doyle. Lillian Craioveneu was exceptionally powerful and keenly deceptive, and her powers would soon be unleashed throughout the entire city. As frightened as these thoughts made her, the fear quickly turned to concern for her husband's safety.

Weaving in and out of lanes, Gloria clutched the steering wheel tighter. "Oh God, what have I done? I'm so sorry, Hugh, I shouldn't have doubted Terry for a second, and now that wicked bitch has her book back," she said aloud as tears welled in her eyes. "Please, God, allow my Hugh to come out of that coma. I need him more than ever."

Gloria knew, from experience, that prayers are rarely answered so quickly, or even at all. Rushing through the hospital, she arrived at Hugh's room at around four o'clock.

"Hello, I'm Gloria McClelland, the patient's wife," she said to the male nurse standing by Hugh's heart and blood pressure monitor with a clipboard. "Has he shown any signs of improvement?"

The nurse peered up from his notes with a subtle smile. "You've just arrived for some good news," he said in an uplifting tone. "Dr O'Hara was round to observe your husband a little over an hour ago and he instructed us to take your husband off the sedation. It seems his breathing is much more in sync and close to the way we want it after we administered the twenty millilitres of ceftazidime to clear his lungs. However, I'm afraid the third degree burn on the side of his face will be permanent."

After the horrendous encounter she had just had, Gloria rejoiced at this piece of news. She clasped her hands together and released an overjoyed smile. "Oh my goodness, thank you so much. I can see his eyelids are flickering. Is he hearing me right now?" she asked, noticing the male nurse's name tag read 'Simon'.

"Funny you should ask, Mrs McClelland," said Simon, glancing at Hugh wrapped in his bandages. "When I observed him before you came in, I'm certain he called out to you and to someone named Daniel. I'm guessing this is another relative of your husband's, yeah?"

"I don't think we know any Daniel, apart from the Jack Daniels he drinks around Christmas while singing Rod Stewart songs," Gloria said, then giggled with joy as she took Hugh's hand in hers and kissed it.

"I see, then. It may just be some delirium brought on by the amount of morphine we have him on. He will require approximately four millilitre doses to keep him comfortable while he recuperates in the ICU for the time being. With the progress he has made so far today, though, that shouldn't be too long. It seems you have a real fighter."

"Thank you, Simon," said Gloria, and hugged the nurse, unable to contain her excitement. "And thank Dr O'Hara and the rest of the staff here. I can't wait to tell the kids their dad is on the right track towards recovery."

"It's been my pleasure, Mrs McClelland. Your husband is very lucky. Looks like he's got someone up there looking out for him."

Gloria looked up towards the ceiling, thinking of Terry. "He's got a best friend up there."

Simon clicked the pen in his hand and returned it to his shirt pocket. "Very well, then, I shall leave you to have your time with him."

"Is there anything I can do?" said Gloria eagerly.

"You're doing it, Mrs McClelland, just by being here. Hold his hand, talk to him, maybe bring a little radio along, if you wish. Perhaps Rod Stewart?" Simon smiled before clipping Hugh's chart back onto the edge of his bed.

Gloria waited until Simon exited the ward before resting her head on her husband's chest as tears of relief ran down her cheekbones, all the while listening to his heartbeat. Holding both his hands in hers, she leaned over to his left ear and whispered, "I'm so sorry this happened to you, my love. I met Terry's demon monster this afternoon and she tricked me into handing over the book. I'm so sorry, Hugh. I was a fool. Who knows what she's going to do?" She leaned closer to his ear. "I'm wishing you a steady and quick recovery, my darling, because as soon as you are back on your feet, together we will begin the hunt for this abomination. To the ends of the earth, wherever her rotten soul hides, we will find her, darling. For you. For me. And for Terry."

Hugh's heart monitor started beeping more frequently, and Gloria glanced over to notice his heart rate increasing from sixty to ninety. Placing her head on his hand, she felt a slight twitch from his fingers as Hugh's eyes slowly opened. They exchanged a silent and stern look filled with purpose, knowing this was not the end of their story, but only the end of the beginning.

About the Author

Paul writes both fiction and local history. Born outside of Glasgow in Paisley he has always been fascinated by the rich history and heritage of his own hometown as well as Glasgow. Spending time studying and researching he always carries his notepad and pen for inspiration.

At eighteen Paul enroled in Paisley University, and although coursework seemed daunting he was inspired and supported by Urban Historian Stephen J. Clancy. His degrees include: University Certificate in Local History, a Heritage Diploma of Higher Education in Creative Writing, and a BA Honours Open Degree from the Open University. In his free time, he enjoys taking his partner Lynsey (and their three children) shopping as well as visiting the cinema at Xscape.

Paul wrote and published three local history books and is delighted with his debut novel, hoping that all his reading audience will enjoy this first novel and the rest to come, thus fulfilling his goal of becoming a full-time author.

Other works by the Author

The Historic West End
Robert Tannahill's Paisley
Medieval Paisley
The Historic Paisley Trilogy

For any other information on other work published please reach out by email at: pauljwandrumauthor@gmail.com

Available on Amazon and Bookstore/Home (jasamipublishingltd.com)

Paul Wandrum